Ba Gua Quan
Foundation Training

By Master
He Jing-Han
disciple of Master Gong Bao Zhai

Lion Books
Taipei, Taiwan

Author/ He Jing Han
Translator/ Yang Ya-Hui
          Alex Kozma
Copyright ©2003 by Lion Books Martial Arts Publishing Company
Published by Lion Books Martial Arts Publishing Company, 3Rm, 9Fl, 57, Chungking South Rd. Sec.1, Taipei Taiwan

ISBN 986-7822-41-2

First edition, 2003
Printed in Taiwan
Distributed by
Taiwan
    www.lionbooks.com.tw
England
    www.lineofintent.com
USA
    tcmedia@tcmedia.com

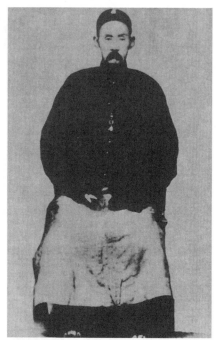

Yin fwu

Yin Yu Jhang

Yin Yu Jhang

Yin Yu Jhang

Gong Bao-Zhai

li- lying down palm
red phoenix facing forward to heaven

due- embracing palm
white ape offers the fruit

jun- supporting palm
green dragon coils upward

kan- downward flowing palm
white snake slithers through the grass

chien- Lion Palm
Name of posture - lion opens his mouth

gang- back palm
black tiger out of the cave

Shing- windmill palm
huge roc opens wings

kuan- Reverse body palm
Chi lin spits the book

CONTENTS

Translator's Introduction

By Alex Kozma

I had been practicing Ba Gua for seventeen years before my first meeting with Master He Jing-Han, and after that memorable lesson from him I began my practice again from zero . His skill in the art, his ability to clearly transmit the most obscure concepts of both martial arts and Chinese culture, was quite simply the highest I had ever encountered. Even more unusual was feeling a deep sense of inner peace and humility about him that completely hid his remarkable internal power. I had found an authentic Ba Gua Quan master.

Being able to work so closely with Master He Jing-Han on the translation of his first book has been a rare chance to deepen my understanding of Ba Gua Quan , and I believe that this book will help all practitioners of the art to throw more light on their own practice . I would like to give you , the reader , a few important notes about the translation work .

First , a little about the presentation of this work and how this was accomplished .

Many of the characters and terms in the original Chinese version of this book are difficult to understand for most modern day Chinese people , even martial arts practitioners .Some of the terms are philosophical concepts , or require one to be practicing the method involved before an understanding of it's meaning is clear . Still other terms - and this is of particular relevance to the reader - are almost impossible to directly translate into English language since they contain depths and shades of meaning that would take perhaps sentences to explain . Can the characters for qi, or jin , for example , be explained by such simple English words as "energy" or "refined force" respectively ? Many translators of Chinese martial arts , philosophical and medical texts have gone this route , sometimes adding glossaries to help the reader understand the various shadings of the original characters .

I recall sitting with Master He one day and asking him about the difference between li and jin , and in reply receiving an hour long explanation on not only their various meanings and applications in the field of martial arts training and philosophy , but also an emphatic caution that Chinese experts often freely inter-changed these terms . In the books of the renowned martial artist Sun Lu Tang, for example, li is sometimes used instead of jin to refer to the same power . Master He continued by saying that yes , he was aware that many had translated li as unre-fined strength , and jin as refined strength , and no , that this was definitely not the case . A cow , for example , is often said to have niu jin (cow's power). Is this crea-ture's strength refined ? Did he practice martial arts in order to refine it ?

Another example that will be of importance to the reader is the translation of zhang as "palm" . Most sources in the English language will directly translate this without further explanation , but it is vital to note that in most cases (at least in this book) zhang actually means "posture" , in other words the shape of the whole body and not just the open hand. Only when specifically referring to the open hand does this zhang refer to the palm . The Ba Mu Zhang , for example , are always translat-ed as "eight mother palms" (which is a correct literal translation) when they are in fact "eight postures". Please bear this in mind in reading this book .

Many Chinese terms can be included in this cautionary note , so we have therefore chosen to keep the original Chinese terms when they fall within this cate-gory (such as - qi, li , jin , yang , yin , Tao , etc....) . To throw some light on these almost-untranslatable terms we have made a glossary at the back of the book which hopefully gives the reader some idea of the possible meanings of the terms. Remember also that even native speakers treat these characters as having many meanings , partly depending on the context and the characters with which they are combined . For those of us working to discover the depths of the Chinese martial arts within ourselves , a contemplation of the original Chinese characters can bring something very useful back into the physical practical.

Secondly , any translation will be to some extent a matter of interpretation of intention as well as syntax , and - as with trying to analyze humor - in the transi-tion from one language to another there is always the danger that something of it's essence may be lost or distorted . To avoid this problem as far as possible , we lived close to master He Jing-Han for two months and spent long hours with him seeking to clarify many of the fine points of the text and the technical terms . Having the good fortune to be his students put us in a position to ask further ques-tions and thus throw even more light on the subject than would have been possible were we removed from the source of the writing. Such an excuse to be with a mas-ter-teacher day in and day out is rare indeed !

Whereas scholars and translators will question the true meaning of a certain word or phrase in Chinese, the disciple of a master-teacher is in the fortunate position of having the true meaning "put" directly into his or her body through subtle postural allignments and by the osmosis which is transmission. Rather than spend two pages debating a concept, we are far better off seeking out a master and asking him to show us directly! One of Master He's most obvious gifts is his ability to strike to the very heart of the concept or subject at hand, and to transmit it's meaning by both example and correction. He told me directly that whilst he respects the martial arts classics , he has made his breakthroughs and attained his realisations through hard work.

Drawing on her study with Master He Jing-Han and a long background in classical Chinese, philosophy and cultivation , Yang Ya-Hui translated the text, which I then put into it's present form . Hopefully this work has managed to convey the true spirit and essence of what Master He was seeking to share in his original writing , but for any inaccuracies I take responsibility for this book and , as the worthies of old said in their tomes , beg the indulgence of the reader.

As the translators we wish to convey our gratitude to Master He Jing-Han for his continuous efforts to pass on the great art form of Ba Gua Quan , to his wife Liza Wu for her support and friendship , to Mr. Lio of Lion Books for his trust in our on-going translation work , and to all of our friends in Taiwan and overseas for assistance and kindness . We especially wish to send deep gratitude to our spiritual master Omram Mikhael Aivanhov for guiding us through this life.

As I have learned from my teachers , the true purpose of martial arts practice - as with all of the ancient art forms - is nothing short of self-mastery and Freedom . We are living on this beautiful spinning jewel in a time when the qualities of authentic wisdom and compassion desperately need to be manifested in each one of us , not just for our own liberation but to prevent the destruction of our magical home . Authentic mind/body practices such as Ba Gua Quan have the deep roots which can nurture such qualities , if one is willing to put in the time and hard work required to reach it's hidden depths .

May all beings be Free !
Alex Kozma , Taipei , Taiwan . March 2003.
Introduction by the translators.

By Yang Ya-Hui

Originally I translated this book due to Alex's enthusiasm for the practice. He knew that this was an excellent book worth studying. I gradually discovered for myself that this was an excellent book from an authentic master.

Master He is a martial arts practitioner with a holistic perspective. You don't find the proud and fierce energy around him, but rather you only find openness and righteousness.

Chinese martial arts has a deep wisdom and meaning just like any real art form. It takes time and your heart to contemplate and study. In this global family what we want to study and transmit is all the experience and advantages from the eastern and western cultures. What we want to discover is the wisdom derived from the Source. Thus we can share the understanding in the present age.

Because of master He's and Alex's sharing and help I benefited a lot from doing this translation. This body follows us every moment and is the best present from God. I believe this book will also benefit many people, and I wish that everyone who has the destiny to read this book will appreciate the beauty of the culture that is inherent in Ba Gua Quan.

Yang Ya-Hui , Taipei , Taiwan. March 2003.

Author's Preface to the English Language Edition

Ba Gua Quan is a mystery - from what we can surmise about it's birth, the stories of the masters, it's innumerable contents, and the variety of styles it has developed until now. To keep the mystery as a mystery is romantic, whilst discovering the mystery is an exploration. Martial arts practitioners take the second way in order to discover the truth.

As with all good explorers, "study" and "action" make a complete exploration. We should know - "why will we do this"? "What are we looking for"? "How can we have a good result"? - before setting out on the journey.

All the contents of this book are based on the teachings of my shrfu , master Gong Bao-Zhai, and I believe that it is the knowledge directly coming from Gong Bao-Tien, Yin Fu, and Dong Hai Chuan. The answers to the three questions above can be found in this book, waiting for the people who really want to know.

Alex Kozma is a martial arts enthusiast, who has spent his life looking for truth. His journey began from a Chinese martial arts book and he knows that many lovers of martial arts need a good book to guide them before they can find a good teacher. I am glad that he chose this book to be the one. He and his lovely wife Yang Ya-Hui spent many days and nights working on it. They traveled around many countries, taking the manuscript and living close to my house for the past two months to ensure that the translation is perfect. Many thanks for their efforts and to Lionbooks martial arts publishing company for making this book come true.

I hope and I believe that this book will help you, although I don't know where and who you are.

Let us link in Ba Gua Quan through this book.

He Jing-Han , Taipei, Taiwan. March 2003.

E-Mail - baguaquan@giga.net.tw

Author's Original Preface

The purpose of martial arts is to enhance human being's happiness . There is a long history of war in China , and traditional martial arts enhanced both the individual and the society until the appearance of the gun and the bomb .

Ever since the end of Ching Dynasty many martial artists still pursued great fighting skill , but there was nobody to fight . Because of this they may have felt isolated , or felt no benefit and happiness.

My study of martial arts has proceeded since senior high school , from Tai Ji Quan , to Xing-Yi Quan , to Ba Gua Quan .

The most valuable attribute of martial arts is the principle that strengthens the ability of the mind and body .

Before the Chou Dynasty martial arts was the practice of the Chinese nobility, helping to cultivate famous leaders who shouldered big responsibility . How abundant are the gifts that your body and mind receive from martial arts - martial arts are not just for fighting !

The essence of Ba Gua Quan is change , and this is also the reality of all Universal phenomena . But how can we know this "change"? There is no certain way . We can only know change from the "unchanging principle". One generates two , two generates three - this is the "unchanging principle". Three generates everything - this is "changeable" .

All things that are clearly seen can be categorized . The wise men investigated this , and from the changeable things they understood the unchanging. so is Ba Gua Quan . Ba Gua Quan teaches unchanging whilst using change . Unchanging is for practicing the ability . The more ability you have to change then the vaster is your ability and the more potential varieties of change you have .

The teaching of Ba Gua Quan is divided into a pre-heaven stage and a post-heaven stage . The pre-heaven stage cultivates skill and is completely unchanging . To apply your skill requires change and this is the post-heaven stage . This introduction and outline of Ba Gua Quan is based mainly on the unchanging and a little on the changing . The introduction of movements is mainly by photographs and a little by writing . The writing by itself is insufficient to explain three dimensional movements .

I consider myself to be a Ba Gua Quan missionary, and wish for people to see the true meaning of martial arts through Ba Gua Quan . My sifu never admitted that he could do martial arts , and I also cannot do martial arts ! We are very fortunate to have this treasure of Chinese culture to joyfully share with everyone , and I am very grateful for the teaching of Gong Bao Zhai for more than twenty years . It is not an easy job for him , especially since I am a lazy and dull student . Thanks also to my wife , that she could stand me regarding martial arts as the number one thing ! Not many people are as fortunate as I am .

My sifu says , "he who can practice doesn't write , he who can write doesn't practice!"

As I am insufficient in both I have to write to give out the knowledge . I welcome any comments from practitioners of other schools who wish to share ideas . This will be the greatest harvest of my work .

He Jing-Han

About the Ba Gua Quan System

Ba Gua Quan became famous in the middle of the Ching Dynasty . Some consider Dong Hai Chuan to be the founder of the system , whereas others consider that he simply transmitted the art . Because of the complex and refined nature of Ba Gua Quan it is clearly not just the creation of a few people during a short period of time .

Dong Hai Chuan was said to be the manager of the Ching Emperor's bodyguards. According to the research of Kang Ge Wu of Beijing , Dong started transmitting Ba Gua Quan at roughly fifty years of age , and it was his top disciple Yin Fu who followed him the longest time and completed learning the whole system . Yin Fu was the teacher of the Ching Emperor's bodyguards .

Gong Bao Tien and his elder brother Gong Bao Shan , both disciples of Yin Fu , were thirty or forty years apart in age . After completing his training, Gong Bao Shan returned to his hometown to be a farmer . In his leisure time he transmitted martial arts to his followers , establishing six small schools where Ba Gua Quan was practiced. Whilst the main schools of Ba Gua Quan were located in the big cities , few of them knew that Gong Bao Shan was a disciple of Yin Fu ; such an occurrence was common in the martial arts field of old times .

When Gong Bao Tien was very young he was recommended by his elder brother to study Ba Gua Quan with Yin Fu . He practiced until sixty years of age and then returned to his home village . During his studies in the Emperor's palace he attained the high forth-rank of bodyguard and wore the yellow robe of such rank . All his life he worked for the Emperor , and hindered by custom he seldom associated with his martial arts brothers who lived outside of the palace. After retiring he went to visit them , but the Ba Gua Quan they had learned was very different and in order to avoid disputes he decided to go home .

Later his brother died from the plague . The disciples of Gong Bao Shan regarded Gong Bao Tien as their second master and continued their practice with him . Whilst both were disciples of Yin Fu , they were quite different - Gong Bao Shan was tall and strong , his martial arts heavy , powerful and stable , whilst Gong Bao Tien was small, thin and weak looking . Gong Bao Zhai described the latter as, "it seemed like the wind could blow him away". His martial arts was light , flexible , vivid , supple and feminine .

My master Gong Bao Zhai learned Ba Gua Quan from an early age with his martial arts brother - a disciple of Gong Bao Shan - and thus learned the heavy , strong way of practice . Later he learned directly from Gong Bao Tien , so he absorbed both ways of the art . His foundation was stable and heavy , but transformed by the light and flexible way . Although he was an inner-door disciple of Ba Gua Quan he seldom associated with martial artists outside of his home village , and thus knew little about other transmissions of the art.

SYNOPTIC TABLE

Generations	Practitioners	Masters
1st	Dong Hai-Chuan	unknown
2nd	Yin Fu	Dong Hai-Chuan
3rd	Gong Bao-Shan, Gong Bao-Tian	Yin Fu
4th	Gong Mao-Zi, Gong Zhan-Shan, Gong Tu-Zi, Gong Bo-Ran, Gong ?-Shuan	Gong Bao-Shan Gong Bao-Tian
	Gong Guan-Yi, Gong Lu-Zhai, Gong Shuang, Gong Bao-Zhai, Gong Yun-Jian, Ho Tian-Guo, Huo Dien-Ge, Li Shin-He, Liu Yun-Chiao,	Gong Bao-Tian
5th	Gong Bao-Gin, Wei Shao-Fu, Chin Hon-Tai, Zhong Shian-Wein, Zhong Dai-Wei, Cui Shang-Wei, Jassy Chang, Michael J. Guen, He Jing-Han, Chou Eugen, Gong Ban-Yan, Huang Jia-Xun, Chou Eshang, Tu Kun-Yii	Gong Bao-Zhai
	Wu-Tang students as their materials	Liu Yun-Chiao
note	1. Gong Bao-Shan's students learned from Gong Bao-Tian after his death, they called Gong Bao-Tian "2nd Sifu". 2. Gong Guan-Yi, Gong Lu-Zhai, Gong Shuang are three sons of Gong Bao-Tian, there are two daughters are good in MA also.	

PART 1. BASIC CONCEPTS

Thought generates belief
Belief generates strength
Concept guides activity
Activity influences concept

Long ago there was a Big Bird and an Owl . Both had the same ancestor , whose mediocre flying skills often meant that they were captured by the Fierce Bird . Thus the sons and grandchildren of this ancestor decided to improve their flying skills . It was something like the story of Jonathon Livingston Seagull , who withstood hunger , cold and loneliness to pursue the skill of flying . These descendent's wings became longer , their chests more powerful , their eyes sharper , their claws stronger , and eventually they evolved to become the Big Bird. The other grandchildren wanted to avoid the threat of the Fierce Bird and chose to abandon the vast sky , hiding in the jungle by night and living off of rotten meat and by eating mice and snakes . Eventually these two became different species , the Big Bird and the Owl .

In the choices of your life there is no right or wrong . But the responsibility of every martial arts practitioner is to improve oneself to higher and higher levels . I hope that every Ba Gua Quan practitioner can become a Big Bird ! Before this , though , it is necessary to have the right concept and thus be able to endure loneliness .

Between heaven and earth
Full of the righteous energy
That flows into every form
Of this material world.
Beneath is river and mountain
Above is the sun and stars
In people is the righteous energy .

Ba Gua Quan Disciplines 1

Deeply conceal your skill as if you have nothing , even though your gong-fu is great .

Always control yourself from showing off . After you have practiced well , and the more emptiness you have attained , conceal your skill even deeper. Do not practice for fighting , for performance , to gain reputation , or even to fight for benefit or fame . Simply practice your inner cultivation . Ba Gua Quan is from Taoism , so these are Taoist words .

Regulate arrogance ! Regulate behavior ! Regulate greed !

First , regulate arrogance . Know that arrogance will stop you progressing , and you will spoil your relationship with other people .

Second , regulate behavior . Too much sex will destroy your virtue and your health.

Third , regulate greed . If you have greed for fame or wealth you will use your skills to deprive others.

If you break these regulations then it is easy to go down the wrong path . Remember that the water which floats the boat also sinks the boat .

Martial Arts are not for Fighting 2

Ba Gua Quan is a process , but you can only really focus on this once you have understood "Wu" . My master often said to me , "you have to learn the principles , not the strength , of martial arts" .

Gong Bao Tien taught that , "martial arts are not for fighting". My master often spoke more, sharing the principles , doing less physical practice with me . He taught me one or two things and would then teach me how to play chess, how to write calligraphy , stories about the great characters from history ....in this way he felt that my martial arts would improve . The way that you deal with people will benefit from this approach , since these arts are all the expressions of a human being"s character and thoughts . We realize that all of the arts are tools and that the ultimate purpose is the person himself.

Is it martial arts if you cannot fight ? Many people would question this . Is it a car if it cannot drive ? Is it an airplane if it cannot fly ? Is it a painting if it cannot be understood ?

Nowadays in the car industry , do they just pursue how fast the car can go ? Does the airplane industry just pursue how high the plane can go ? Does the clothing industry just make clothes which will keep you warm ? In the art field , do people only make paintings which depict a real scene ?

The purpose of martial arts is to cultivate life . Although it's primary method is fighting , for thousands of years Chinese martial arts and Chinese culture have mingled with each other . Of course you can fight using martial arts , but then it is only win or lose . Of course you can make your body strong by doing martial arts , but then you will simply be healthy until your death . But without doing martial arts we can still fight and still be healthy . If you do martial arts for these reasons you neglect the truth of Chinese martial arts . Thus I continue to speak my master's words........

"Martial arts are not for fighting!"

Ancient Martial Artists 3

Although the origins of the martial arts cannot be fully known , we can say that it was fully developed during the Chou Dynasty . The education of the nobility was based on "scholar way and martial way unified" (wen wu her ee). This was in order to give them the ability to protect the land in wartime , and to manage the land and control the citizens during peacetime . After the decline of the Chou Dynasty many great people and martial arts experts emerged and the next generation of nobility had expertise in both the scholar arts and the martial arts . This was normal for their class, but even amongst the ordinary folk there were some great practitioners and countless folk heroes . Such people also had the ability to kill an enemy from horseback , along with literary skills .

It is said that ,"it takes ten years to cultivate a tree , but a hundred years to cultivate a person".

These heroes and arts , from which school or teacher or method did they come? Beneath it all was the long period of the education system based on "scholar way and martial way unified". After the her-ju exam (the imperial examination) of the Ching and Han Dynasty, scholar arts and martial arts separated and nobody could excel at both . Thus people could not manage events of the world very well . Even back in the Ming Dynasty and the proceeding Dynasties , however , the people still studied both ways equally. Thus , whenever an emergency befell the land , if the officials did not know how to respond then a hero would emerge from the common folk in order to help .

Ba Gua Quan derives from Taoism , and it has spread to the world since Dong Hai Chuan became the transmitter . It was transmitted to the third generation - Gong Bao Tien - and from the palace to the countryside . It's teaching still maintains "scholar way and martial way unified" , since it's root is the human being. This ideal and practice is worth studying, for both the scholar and the martial artist .

Officially martial arts was set by the course of events . Every one learned different things but all had the duty of the martial way .

Ordinary martial arts had many branches because their aims were different .

Some heroes protected rich people . Some were hired as assassins . Some were rascals. Their aims and ways were different , and these became the various castes of martial arts society .

No matter whether you are of the nobility or the common folk , if you learn scholar arts or martial arts , it is said , "If you learn from the highest you can only succeed in the middle , if you learn the middle level the fruits are even lower !". No matter whether you teach or practice you have to pay attention to this point .

"Scholar Way and Warrior Way Unified" (wen wu her ee)

4

The human body contains intelligence and force, and life contains wen (scholar Way) and wu (martial Way). The growth of human beings is "force first, then intelligence after" , thus the old Greek saying "a healthy mind relies on a healthy body". This is deeply significant . The ancient Greeks cultivated their people both externally and internally through the practice and promotion of the Olympic games , so they developed such an excellent Greek civilization. The prosperity or decline of China is always associated with the practice of contemporary "wen wu her ee". On the surface scholar arts are closer to intelligence , and martial arts are closer to strength, so the study of calligraphy is wen , riding the horse and bow and arrow is wu. But actually out of wu you develop the thinking , the ability , the personality. However, wen is the expression of this thinking, ability and personality. For example, playing the zither (stringed instrument), chess, calligraphy and painting can also be wu. Riding a horse and practicing bow and arrow can also be wen.

Ritual, music, bow and arrow skills, horse riding, scriptures, maths - these six arts were the curriculum of study in the academy of Zhou dynasty and were adopted by Confucius. Ritual was done in order to discipline the body, as were the basic stances in the martial arts. Music had the function of harmonizing the mind, just like forms in martial arts. Bow and arrow shooting was to learn how to apply the body to control external objects, just like staff, spear, saber and sword in martial arts. Horse riding was to learn how to apply your body and mind to control the external living things, as with two-person practice in martial arts. Calligraphy was to learn how to express the way to write. Maths was for everyday living, for calculation. So the first four arts belong to the training of wu, and the last two are the application of wen. We know that wu is not only the training basis of wen but also the training basis for human beings.

Yes, this is the spirit of "Scholar Way and Martial Way Unified" ! This is also the basic concept of Ba Gua Quan's teaching.

Knowledge and Wisdom 5

Knowledge is from outside and is easy . Wisdom is cultivated from inside and is difficult . The key point is understanding . The traditional masters didn't easily talk about key points - if the student had a question they would simply say, "Practice!" . Very occasionally they would speak , and the student would keep the master's words in his heart his whole life . Students actively received knowledge and a good foundation. Nowadays however , information spreads very fast , and before learning students have already read many books . After learning, students take the knowledge as a reference, so now the master has to explain things . It is the student who decides what kind of knowledge he wants or doesn't want .

"Many sounds make the ears deaf , many colours make the eyes blind".

Most students have much knowledge but do little practice and action . The purpose of knowledge is to cultivate wisdom and you will only do this if you have faith . In the process of cultivation , if there are any obstacles or questions then you may try to search out the answer so you can adjust your thoughts. From understanding you hear one thing and know ten things . You hear a shallow point and know a deep point . If knowledge is absorbed too quickly then there is no time to digest it , and it will simply be rubbish in the brain . This rubbish becomes more and more until the student is very difficult to teach , and finally he may have enough knowledge to fill five cars but he still has no wisdom .

"When heaven gives man a big mission he makes him hungry and makes his body suffer. when your heart wants to act , control your instinct , and this may improve what you cannot yet do" . If we can bear suffering then we will improve our ability a little. Dr. Sun Yut San considered that there are three types of understanding - that which is inborn , that which is learned , and that which is extracted from the result of suffering . Martial arts education goes from body to mind and is of the third type .

Adjust your concepts little by little , contemplate what you understand . Nothing can be rushed. If there is any question then find the answer by yourself. A master can only show you the direction, and using this concept is the way to teach .

Unchanging and Changing 6

The essence of Ba Gua Quan is changing.

It is said that, "Changing is the only truth of unchanging in the Universe."

There should be some roots and principle for any kind of changing, and these roots and principles are the unchanging. Changing itself cannot be directly understood or studied, so if you want to know it and even direct it then the only way is through unchanging.

Ba gua is unchanging. The ancient wise men watched and investigated nature, and from deductive reasoning found ba gua. But si xiang, liang yi, taiji - these are the roots reasoned from ba gua. "Taiji generates liangyi , liangyi generates si xiang, si xiang generates ba gua. We use this word "generate", not "change", just like parents generate their children, not "parents change into their children".

"Taiji", "liangyi", "si xiang", "ba gua", is a model. It analyses the yin yang energy which is formless but with substance, from the endless chaos energy. Then this yin yang energy is distributed to the si xiang (four images), which is without substance but with form. Finally this generates ba gua which has both form and substance. Ba gua is full of potential that is preparing to generate a thousand worlds. Ba gua is the mother of changing, and it is unchanging.

Ba Gua Quan is the martial art which corresponds with ba gua. Through the image of ba gua contemplate the form of si xiang and the substance of liang yi. From this point return to the chaos of taiji. Then you extrapolate your own ba gua. Thus you complete the Ba Gua Quan journey from unchanging to changing.

Essence and Function 7

Essence is unchanging and is the basis of function. Function is changing and is the extension and application of essence. An example of this is the relationship between basic science and applied science. Ba gua is unchanging, and it also comprises eight basic essences . The sixty four hexagrams are changing, and are derived from the eight basic essences - such as mountains , medical science , physiognomy , reading one's fate and so on . They are from the same essence but with different applications.

What is the common basic ability of human beings? And what kind of common basic ability do we need for application? What kind of person will be cultivated by training? Modern knowledge has various levels of education. The specialist technical school is especially for training technicians and it can generate immediate benefit. But the technical academy level is higher, since it trains the technician who has the ability to grow and to extend the development of the field. University education trains a group of useless people in a positive way - their thinking is very broad but they have no specialization. But if they go further and study at doctor level then their accomplishment will certainly surpass that of the technicians.

Chuang Tze said, "that which is useless has the greatest use".

The future development of a country and society is handled by useless people. A martial arts teacher can train a group of fighters to protect the country, and even to protect their schools . He can also train a group of martial arts teachers to build up and expand their schools. But the real martial arts education is to educate an authentic and complete person. This is a real disciple and a real inheritance. The only purpose of martial arts training is to extract the complete potential of the student. The ultimate purpose is the students themselves, and they shouldn't have any desire of benefits.

To cultivate technical specialists needs from two to four years to see results. To cultivate an undergraduate or even a doctor needs about eight years. No need to say how long we may have to wait for his invention, so often the learning is hurried and the teacher has no patience. There are millions of soldiers but it is hard to find a good general. Martial arts is the training process from body to mind, leading to union of body and mind , during which we not only learn discipline and develop the body and mind but also will develop a multidirectional thought pattern.

People who are qualified to have this ability will have great use. They can be either scholar or martial artist, either a farmer or an officer, either materialistic or renounced, either good or evil.

Some people say that martial arts forms are useless, some say that they are useful and that they focus on merging the sequences of postures . Actually all martial arts schools sequences of postures are for training the essence , and this is also true of Ba Gua Quan .

Sequence , Posture , Forms. 8

Forms are valuable like a program of music.

A posture is a static directional body structure with dynamic potential.

Some postures seem to go in only one direction, but actually the surrounding space is taken care of by the eyes , mind and body in all directions .

One posture is like the ranks of soldiers in a battle.

A sequence is a series of complete advancing and retreating movements.

1 sequence can have 1 posture.

1 sequence can have 2 postures .

1 sequence can have 4 postures.

The effect of the sequence is a result of the changing flow of the shr (the force). So no matter the combination, these changing movements should be completed within the space of a single breath . No matter how powerful your combination, finally it will become one posture as light as the wind.

Forms are a combination of sequences. The flowing energy should be unified and penetrate between the sequences making the form have it's own unique style. When you practice a form you should contemplate its deep meaning. You cannot be like the little monk who chanted the prayers by his mouth but not with his heart. Of course you can recite, then understand, and still gain some effect from it.

Staff , Saber , Spear , Sword. 9

"Empty-hand forms" are for developing the body and mind, enabling you to contemplate the body and mind's interaction, the principles of exercise, and the mystery of energy, through progressive training. Through this training you can effectively use your body and mind.

"Staff, saber, spear, sword" - these are the four main weapons honored by martial art practitioners. This is the necessary next stage for the traditional practitioner who has the good basis of empty hand forms.

Some people say, "in this present age, with all the guns and bombs available, is it worthwhile to practice these classical weapons?"

The teaching of Confucius emphasized the six arts - "ritual, music, bow and arrow, horse riding, calligraphy and math". Ritual and music was for the body and mind. After you can handle and control your body and mind, then you study how to control the external objects with this basis. So "staff, saber, spear, sword" are the "bow and arrow" of Confucius teaching but even more complete and complex.

These four weapons contain two which are steel-like and two which are supple, two heavy and two light, two long and two short, two single and two pairs.

Staff - contributes steel-like strength, and is a heavy and long weapon with double head. It is used with both hands and applied mainly by the shoulder. The force goes horizontally, the footwork mainly focuses on stable stepping with few changes.

Saber - this contributes steel-like strength and is a heavy short weapon with a single-sided blade. It is used with one hand but demands a balanced force from both hands. It mainly uses the elbow and shoulder, and the force goes horizontally, with stable steps and few changes.

Spear - this contributes supple force, it is light and long with a single head used by both hands. Moved by the shoulder, elbow and wrist together, but mainly focused on the wrist. Most of the force is vertical and vortex-like , with the steps being very light, agile and with many changes.

Sword - this contributes supple force, it is a light short weapon with double blade. Held by one hand, but this time the shoulder , elbow and wrist are used. This has both steel-like and supple qualities . The movements are like a snake, agile and changeable. The force is vertical and vortex-like. The arms are moved by the waist, the steps are agile and changing without limits. In this way you can express the great harmony of human being and weapon.

From the above we can see that the four weapons each has it's own special characteristic, feature and mood. This is completely expressed by each one's own form. So "staff, sabre, spear, sword" is actually for the purpose of studying the nature of different objects.

These four weapons use includes all the traditional weapons usage. If the practitioner can harmonize his own nature and the objects nature then what he learns is far more than just the weapons.

Qi, Li , Skill. 10

Qi is energy, with no form , no shadow , omni-present . The flow of qi generates li .The change of li generates skill. The movement of skill leads the qi. This is a simple and also complex relationship. Human beings have qi - this is the life force which we originally have (pre-heaven qi) or which we cultivate (post-heaven qi). If your qi is strong then you are strong. If your qi is weak then you are weak. However, the strength or weakness of the qi doesn't rely on the quantity but on whether or not the qi is gathered and unified.

"Lead the qi by li, control the li by qi".

These are the two initial stages of Ba Gua Quan , and should be the mutual method of internal and external cultivation .

Qi is stored in the body chaotically and without order, just as water in a lake has no specific direction. Suppose we offer it direction by an external force, then water gathers and becomes a flow which we can then use to generate electricity. In this way the water can generate a certain effect. qi is scattered in the body randomly just like cows scattered in a field, until the farmer can lead the cows with a rope and set them to work on the field or pulling a wagon.

The early stage of li is derived from muscles, tendons and movement. "Leading the qi by li" - this is the leading force generated by the gestures of the four limbs from external to internal. Different gestures create forces in different directions.

By this force you can create a flowing path for the body's energy to flow from internal to external, so that the qi in the body can follow this path and become an active flowing energy which can be utilized.

"Leading the qi by li" - if we take the hand as the starting point and seek the terminus internally, then as long as the path is clear qi will be like flowing water generating a flowing internal force . Then we should take the terminus as the originating point to motivate the internal force by leading the qi. This is the stage of "controlling the li by qi".

"Stiffness is the biggest thing that will block the flowing path of energy". Thus every school responds by saying "relax!".

Ba Gua Quan also proclaims the need for relaxation. This is because only in a relaxed state can you deeply twist your tendons and muscles, and stretch the sinews. In this way the limbs and body, and the internal and external , are practically connected . Only after the training of twisting and stretching until the state of "controlling li by qi", the muscles can really be relaxed .

The stage of "leading the qi by li". The body moves in order to maintain the specific forces and directions to create a path , and this stage is very monotonous , until "qi and li are unified" will produce different levels of variation . The body moves from stillness and develops different postural sequence skills , and in this way they will lead different flows of qi and li and the expression of martial art skill will have colorful variations .

The Mystery of Force. 11

Originally I didn't understand why martial arts education was so vital for cultivating the future leaders in the old times.

Practicing martial arts can strengthen your body, train your mind , enhance your wisdom , protect country and family - these are the necessary criteria for the old time leaders. Why did the elite of society possess such holistic ability as a result of their martial arts education? What did they understand or realize? What did they possess?

Afterwards I discovered that one of the most vital purpose of studying martial arts is "li" (force) . Everything in the Universe is full of the expression of li. Actually everything is constantly moving and movement generates force, so the only element which permeates all the things in the Universe is li . If you can control the law of li then you can control the movement of everything. Martial arts education - in terms of the study of "li" which is concealed in every stage of training , concealed in every movement - adopts the method of self-understanding through overcoming obstacles. The study objects and tools are you yourself. Every joint's angle and position; tendons, bones and muscles twisting , contraction or extension ; the shifting of the body's center of gravity ; the relative relationship between limbs , head , shoulders and back , waist , kwa , knees ; the focus of the eyesight ; the concentration of the mind ; the thoughts you project or receive ; the concept of attack and defend ; internal energy closes and opens , and travels up and down - all of these things influence the orientation of li in every posture and sequence . If any one of these things change then it will effect the focus of li, and any change of li will naturally change all of these things.

A human being's microcosm conceals the underlying principle of the vast and refined macrocosm. The practitioner contemplates the inter-relationship and types of li, starting by adjusting the li in his own body. He contemplates the formation of li by the static posture. He contemplates the flow of li by active martial arts forms. He contemplates the primary and secondary li through the practice of weapons. He contemplates the inter-response of li through two-person practice.

Step by step, year-by-year, this contemplation makes the practitioner become immersed in the life of li. Then he is able to cultivate a sensitivity and response to li, and in this way the practitioner instinctively discovers that behind everything is a basic motivating force. By knowing the one you know the hundred. You make the complicated become simple.

Limbs and Body. 12

The human body has three major lines - one connecting the shoulders (horizontal), one connecting the kwa (horizontal, hip joints area), and also the spine (vertical). The basic principle of most movements is to keep these lines level.

The body can be separated into two parts - the thorax and abdomen. The thorax consists of twelve ribs which, like a mother protecting her baby, protect the heart and lungs. The heart and lungs are directly connected with the spine. The stomach, large and small intestines, liver , spleen and kidneys all float in oil and water . The mid-section can move up and down, it's muscles can extend and retract, thus changing the pressure of each body part. How is this done? By the limbs. From the layout and function of the torso we can see that the body is the base of life energy - if there are no limbs we still can live. If energy cannot circulate, obstacles will repeatedly come to us and cause excess pressure on our organs. The limbs create movement and space for energy to be balanced and circulated. If the energy of the body can flow to the limbs, then the limbs and body will be unified by that energy. The link for this flow is the area of the shoulder blades and the kwa . They are the most important gates but also the easiest to be obstructed.

The more refined the motion of the limbs, the deeper the effect in the body .

Body and Mind. 13

Body, mind and spirit are the three elements of existence of all human beings. The body is the human being's physical state. It can be analyzed, it can be sensed, it can be seen. Mind is the human's mental state, so contemporary science can also estimate it's nature. Spirit is the origin of life, and it belongs to the domain of religion. There is no way to measure it and thus no certain conclusion about it.

The contents of martial arts include body and mind, but many grandmasters also went into the pursuit of spirit. That is the inevitable result after practice and cultivation of the heart and mind. Martial arts just lead people to the Way.

The changes of the body can be sensed and practiced , so the body is easy to handle. It is the indispensable basis for the cultivation of body, mind and spirit.

The inter-dependence of body and mind was not proved by science until the twentieth century, but long before this Chinese medicine considered that, "liver conceals a wandering spirit(huen), lungs conceal a wandering spirit(pao), heart conceals a wandering spirit(shen), kidney conceals the will, spleen conceals yi". So we know that there is an absolute relationship between the biological and psychic state of human beings. Ba Gua Quan not only concedes this but also takes it as the content of its essential training.

People say, "you are what you eat" , and also "what you practice you will look like". Eating habits will influence a human beings character, and the exercise habit will have even more influence, especially martial arts since it is a serious practice over a long period during which your mind and heart will be involved. "What you train", "how you train it", both these things influence you very, very deeply.

The violent systems of martial arts will train violent people. Cruel systems will train cruel people, and flirtatious systems will train flirtatious people. The generous system will train generous people. This influence has something to do with blood and energy and also mentality. This is the key point for training people with martial arts and is also the point of Ba Gua Quan"s precept "train the heart by the body".

The refinement of body involves using the heart and mind for it's understanding, and the movement of heart/mind has to be provided and cultivated by the body. Body is yang, heart/mind is yin. If you neglect this and directly cultivate your heart and mind, this is like building a tower on the sand. The body and heart/mind will always have conflicts and the root will be very fragile. If you only emphasize the training of the body, but neglect the cultivation of the heart, this is like the horse without the reigns. It is hard to control the wildness, and easy to lose the way in violence. Moreover, the potential of your body cannot be sufficiently expressed. So train yin and yang in harmony, train both body and heart/mind , in this way you will achieve smoothness and balance. This is the real way to practice martial arts , and this concept is also the foundation of spiritual cultivation.

Jin and Li. 14

There are many sources of li in martial arts. Muscles tense and relax, the sinews flex, the body advances and retreats , the inhalation and exhalation of the breath, the concentration of the yi - all of these elements integrate and correspond with each other to produce jin. If you tense a muscle it becomes tight, if you relax it then it becomes long. If the tensing and relaxation is strong enough then you will develop the sinew's flexibility, and no matter whether you are retreating or advancing then you will have smooth movement. Also the breathing will be very smooth and the mind focused. Thus relaxation is the common principle of many martial arts.

Ba Gua Quan lengthens muscles by utilizing many twisting movements, and trains the sinew's flexibility which thus enhance the agility of the joints, using a level of refinement which includes all the joints from those as small as fingers to those as big as hips.

The movements in Baguaquan rely strongly on "steps". The steps move like walking only acting from the relaxed legs and hip joints - this will make the movements flexible, agile and stable.

There are two kinds of breath in Baguaquan, one cooperates with movements for enhancing health while the other one is isolated from movements in fighting. Both of them need a deep , long and directed breath . Different kind of breathing generates different kinds of power.

The mind in Baguaquan practice is from focused to empty - actually the empty comes from focus, and the focus in movements is from the outside of the body towards the inside.

There is only one "jin" in Baguaqun, called " self-coming jin". It will come by itself if the training process is completed. "Jin" is a kind of power like a tank of water - we can utilize the water pressure in many methods, but the source is the same.

Therefore don't look for "jin" - jin will come to you if your body is ready.

Smooth , Connected ,Level , Balanced.

15

The circulation of nature , no matter in heaven or on earth or in anything at all, has as its function the maintenance of smoothness and balance.

The Tao of human beings existence, no matter in body, mind or the relationship of objects, also consists of smoothness and balance, and no matter for body or mind or the skills, the training of Ba Gua Quan has this as it's goal. "Smooth" means no obstacles. "Balanced" means not going to extremes. If a human being's body and mind are without obstacles and don't go to extremes, then that person really has wisdom, freedom and omnipotence. But what a pity that everybody confines themselves in habits and discriminations and thus destroys their body and mind's smoothness and balance. Finally, because of this, they cannot even control their own bodies.

Ba Gua Quan itself is a smooth and balanced combination. Each of the eight posts has it's own position. The yin and the yang nourish each other. When Ba Gua Quan relates to the human body, "liang yi" represents left and right, up and down, internal and external; "si xiang" represents the four limbs and the eight joints; and Ba Gua represents the systems of the heart, lungs, liver, kidney, head, back, waist and abdomen, thus constructing a complete system of internal cultivation and external training.

A complete training system is relevant to "Are the contents in balance?", but how to train to achieve smoothness and balance is even more important. In the process of practicing Ba Gua Quan you cannot over-emphasize one aspect of training.

The real process of Ba Gua Quan teaching is very complex and time consuming, very changeable. "Qi and li", "li and wisdom", "Body and Mind", "Internal and External", "stillness and suppleness", "stability and agility" , "up and down", "theory and skill", "changing and unchanging", even the tendons, bones, muscles and joints of every part of the body, all of these are two sides of one scale. In the process of training you should actively adjust and change from one to the other. Don't over train one aspect, or one kind of force, or else the smooth circulation of the qi and the blood will be blocked.

My master Gong Bao Zhai once said, "One master can only teach three to five real disciples in his lifetime". This is because if you really want to take disciples the cost is very high.

Can practicing your martial art give you health and longevity?

Can practicing your martial art enhance your existence?

Can practicing your martial art improve your life?

This all depends on whether the practitioner gradually inclines towards balance and smoothness, or on the other hand accelerates the destruction of these qualities.

Practitioners! Be careful!

Medical Science, Physiology , Theory of Practice.

Medical science , physiology and the theory of practice - these are the three elements of Ba Gua Quan and any posture or movement should match these three criteria. Physiology means the construction of the human body. No matter if the practitioner is a strong young man, old or weak, woman or child, the key point of practice and the movements will be different depending on their physiology and so it cannot be generalized.

The principle of physiology is "qi and blood go together", "intelligence and yi correspond to each other". If the practitioner only perceives the beauty of the performance or the use of fighting, it is unavoidable that he or she will make some forceful movements during practice. In this way their qi will oppose the correct flow and their blood flow will be blocked, thus hurting their physiology. It is the inevitable result of lack of correspondence between body and mind.

Young men are full of strength and energy, their qi and blood is very powerful, so they can easily express the steel-like and quick movements. But when the same skills are practiced by the middle-aged master, it will look natural, supple and smooth. This is not due to the different schools.

Medical science is the theory of adjusting the body and mind in order to be smooth and balanced. Everyone's physiological and psychological development has some weakness, and therefore cannot be balanced and smooth. The purpose of all medical methods is how to correct the weakness, how to adjust the strong parts, and how to balance the strong and weak parts.

Ba Gua Quan leads the qi and blood intentionally by movement. It is based on the principle of the five elements. The key point is the "mother and son" theory which seeks to adjust the relationship between all the organs. Each organ , according to it's construction and essence , will have it's own refined training.

Practitioners of Ba Gua Quan will gradually have the awareness of their organs, blood, qi, and the movement of their tendons and bones, after a long period of careful and refined practiced. In addition, practitioners will be able to adjust the weak and strong parts of their body through the theory of skill. Then they can achieve the level of being balanced, centered and upright in mind and body. This is the method and purpose enabling the practitioner to realize medical science.

When you project outwards the movements of Ba Gua Quan, it contains two meanings. "Outwardly for defense, inwardly for cultivation." So Ba Gua Quan has both sides and you cannot lack either one of them. It is not only for fighting, and it is not only for cultivation.

The movements and the postures of the martial arts have qi and li, and Ba Gua Quan uses this to lead and influence the inner organs and the flow of blood and qi. Different forces will lead different types of qi, different organs, and different jin-lo (jin paths). It is easy to say but when you practice this it is very detailed and refined. There is one saying - "before the wind blows the bug knows, before the moonlight has reflected on the twig the bird has already flown." If you can be as sensitive as this, neither internal cultivation nor external application will not present a difficulty.

Training and Maintenance 17

The purpose of training is to make iron become steel, to make coal become diamond.

After maintenance iron is still iron, only now it does not rust, and coal is still coal but now you don't make it into soot.

Should human beings do training or maintenance? Ba Gua Quan has both.

Martial art practitioners generally train with martial arts but not in maintenance. Their common concept is to train what you cannot yet do. Train to be good at what you are not good at, and to strengthen what is weak. Training is the practitioners whole life but not every practitioner has longevity. Many highly skilled practitioners passed away early in life. This is relevant to the principle of "balanced and smooth" , and also because they lost the balance of maintenance and training.

Everyone's pre-birth body has "essence", and the post-birth environment is different, but generally speaking before middle age we should emphasize on training more than maintenance , and after middle age maintenance more than training. But if you have a weak body, even if you are eight years old still you have to maintain first and then train . So these are the two sides of the scale which we should consider.

Once I was scolded by my master because I made my fist calloused. He said, "martial art training is to benefit the body, but you hurt yourself before you benefit it."

Some trees grow only a little bit each year, and after many years they are of very good quality. Some trees grow very tall in one year, but after that they are useless. Human beings maturity and ability should be little by little, accumulating from inside to outside.

This is a saying, "if you want the tree to grow very tall you must make the roots go very deep. If you want the river to go very far, you have to make sure the source is potent."

Ba Gua Quan has inner cultivation and external training. The early period leads the inner cultivation by external training : that is the stage of "leading the qi by li", with the focus on steel-like power. The latter period harmonizes internal cultivation and external training. This is the stage of "control the li by qi". It's attributes are supple. Every form can use the early and latter periods , and can be used for maintenance and training , depending on the practitioners criteria and the teacher's intentions.

Practitoner, if you only know "train hard, train hard, train hard", and practitioner, if you only know fighting - I want to remind you that Chang San Feng (the founder of Tai Ji Quan) said , "I hope that all practitioners have longevity and good health , and won't be the slave of the skill."

After all, wu is for life, not for death.

Specialization and Generalization 18

Specialization is deep but narrow. Generalization is broad and abundant. Exploring endless knowledge by limited life , wanting to be both broad and deep - this is not easy. Ancient practitioners often spent their whole life following one thing. Thus many people were good at one school, good at one form, good at one weapon, good at one scripture, like General Gwan's saber, Zhang Fei's long spear, Yang family's spear. They loved what they were good at, harmonized with what they loved , and were inseparable from that.

Specialization and generalization is not only a method but also an attitude. That is to say, through specialization and generalization different methods will produce different attitudes and thinking. Specialization is a deep level of study. Students will not be satisfied with the superficial meaning of the subject so they pursue it inwardly, and the further they pursue it inwardly the deeper they go, and the more deep they go then the more excited and surprised and joyful they feel. At last they see the origin of everything, understanding the genes which control everything. So this specialization becomes a person's base, and he stands on this base and can see through the essence of things which are colorful and complex.

Every school has it's basic forms. The practitioners have to practice very deep, and after they realize something they can go to the next step. This is the meaning of specialization first and generalization after.

It is said that in the past there was an opera group. There was an experienced actor who could play any kind of role or drama when they were short of actors, but if you asked him to play the main role he could not do it. "Eighteen kinds of martial arts, everyone you know , everyone you know little."

This is not only a regulation for martial arts practitioners. Teachers are also like this. Having lots of students was an insult not an honor to the ancient traditional martial arts masters, because martial arts teaching involved many things. There is a saying, "transmitting the skill is easy, but transmitting the heart is difficult, and the heart means the thought and conception". If the students only want to be like the actor we mentioned above, and if the students cannot surrender themselves, even a teacher having very high skill cannot transmit what he has to his disciple. How many masters when they are alive teach lots of students, but after death they have nobody to take their transmission forward.

Martial arts is transmitted by human beings. If the people are alive then the art is alive. If the people are dead then the art is dead. So the idea of "general transmission or specialized transmission" takes time to deeply consider and contemplate.

Faith and Doubt 19

The life of any religion consists of faith . Have faith in your guru , scripture , heaven and hell , in good spirits and bad spirits , in the ability to change the elements of wind and rain , on being able to bi-locate (having two bodies) - all of these illogical things which cannot be examined are taken as true.

If a religion cannot have a disciple of complete faith then this religion would be declared to be dead . Do you believe that human beings can walk on the roof and on water , walk one thousand miles a day , and be invulnerable to weapons ?

If there is no faith , there is no surrender . How can you study sincerely without surrender ? If there is no faith in the teacher , then there is no faith in the martial art's skills and it is dead . This being the case , who benefits from faith , and who receives the disadvantage from doubt ? What would you lose if you have faith ? What can you obtain if you have doubt ? You are afraid that you will get hurt so you have doubt . But by having a doubtful mind you have already hurt yourself .

There is an old saying that as long as I believe that I can do something , then the day will come when I shall complete the most difficult of tasks - such as moving a mountain , or reclaiming the land from the sea . Yet if I don't have faith then I cannot even do the easiest things such as turning my palm or breaking a twig .

The right attitude towards pursuing the truth is "believe first , then question , then find the answer." If you have doubt and then afterwards try to believe , faith will never come . The essence of martial arts is to train what you cannot do until you can do it . The union of body , mind and soul is a pursuit of the unknown. The unknown cannot be proved or interpreted , so seek the unknown and overcome what you cannot do . The key point of your success or failure is doubt and belief , and this is the most difficult thing in the contemporary teaching of martial arts . You cannot have slight doubt in your faith , or else that is not faith. What a difficult thing for smart , scholarly modern people !

The Self Confidence of Martial Artists

20

In Ba Gua Quan the regulations are against arrogance, greed and lust !

There is a saying , " There is no first amongst scholars , in martial arts there is no second !"

More or less every practitioner will consider their transmission and skill as the best one . In fact if this was not the case then the martial artist could not follow his school and transmission for such a long time and train very hard , so it is this that can necessarily lead them into arrogant . Moreover, mostly it comes from the confidence of the practitioner themselves . Because of their ability gained through long effort they completely understand what they can and cannot do . This confidence can easily become arrogance, and ultimately it can become the arrogance of the "frog in the well" perspective .

So , this is the first regulation of Ba Gua Quan .

When practitioners have small achievements and gradually contact with others , he will discover that others have also grown through lots of hard work and by overcoming frustration . The mature artist will start to learn to respect other's hard work . So arrogance becomes tolerance , consideration and appreciation . Finally all that is left is the practitioner's confidence in himself .

The most precious asset of a martial artist is confidence , and it is the original source of courage which enables him to face any challenge . Through training you can cultivate your ability - this kind of concept is stored in every cell of the practitioner's body and stored in his mind . This perception is gained not through study but through hard training . Lots of martial artists consider themselves a hero , as we see in history . Some succeeded , some failed , but this spirit is unique to the martial arts practitioner . I have seen that some ancestors of martial arts practitioners were not afraid of ghosts or spirits . When difficulties came they overcame them . When illness came they cured themselves . It is not that they did not want to get assistance from the doctor , spirit or destiny - it is just that they were instinctively unwilling to hand over the responsibility for themselves to others .

Being responsible for your own life is the irreplaceable character of the martial artist.

The Vast Compassion of Martial Artists

21

Wen Wu Her Ee (scholar Way and warrior Way unified)

Martial arts are for protecting people, not for killing . The mission of the practitioner is to protect people, not to kill them. Low level martial artists use violence to fight violence, and the low class practitioner stops killing by killing. Old time martial arts and martial artists , however, were far away from this attitude. We don't have to talk about this through theory, and there is no need to analyze the aspiration of the hero to save the whole world. Simply by reading the seven classic martial arts books we can understand that the mutual idea is to have an overwhelming army which stops the war before it starts .

From the high peak of Chinese martial arts emerged Tai Ji Quan and Ba Gua Quan . Tai Ji Quan focuses on softness , following and yielding . Ba Gua Quan is very agile and changeable - it's highest skill is "entwining palm", in which you consider your enemy as your lover and entwine together with him . There were several times when my Grandmaster Gong Bao Tien was forced to fight , but at the most he only made a hole in the adversary's clothing . Moreover , he covered the tear so that no one could see it , in order to save the face of the other person . Other schools have similar stories about their masters . The essence of what these masters learned from their whole life is "protecting themselves , but not hurting others" . We can see this intention even in the four main weapons of Chinese martial arts , the staff, saber , spear and sword .

Staff - the intention of the staff is to avoid killing people , so the method is based on "sweep" and "peck" . Therefore it has no blade or sharp point .

Spear - this has only the point but no blade . The method is mainly "prick" , and it's purpose is to control the adversary's joints . So it's purpose is not for killing.

Saber - only one side is a blade and the point is sharp . Moreover only the top section of the blade is sharp . The method is "slice" not hack , so it is not for killing .

Sword - this has a single point and double blade . Only the point and three inches down are used . The method is "pierce through" , not kill .

These four main weapons can kill but actually they are not used for killing. When you practice with them you must have a very peaceful mind with no hint of violence , and this will make the energy very smooth . In Chinese martial arts if you don't practice your inner cultivation and morality , and have no love , at the most you are just a killer and will never have a glimpse of the splendor of this art .

It is said , " it is easy to kill , difficult to hurt . Easy to hurt , difficult to catch . Easy to catch , difficult to make them surrender ." The heart of love and compassion makes the body soft and supple . The energy of violence and stubbornness makes the body stiff and hard . The development of Chinese martial arts is from very hard to supple , and this orientation has a great intention behind it . Modern practitioners need to contemplate and understand this very carefully , and avoid going the other way around .

PART 2. A BROAD DDECRIPTION OF THE BA GUA QUAN SYSTEM

A broad description of the Ba Gua Quan system is shown in the table . The Eight Mother Palms postures and the Eight Palms are the heart of the entire system . The two basic forms "ba gua zhang" and "ba gua quan" are the basis for application . The sequence shown in the chart is not necessarily the sequence for teaching the system .

As for the categorization of qi, li , Internal , and External - this is only to express the essence . Ba Gua Quan is changeable and so don't get stuck in the terms .

BA MU ZHANG POSTURES
Single Change Palm
Double Change Palm
Snake Palm
Hook Palm
Closing Palm
Downward flowing Palm
Returning back Palm
Embracing Palm

EIGHT PALMS
Lion Palm
Downward flowing Palm
Reverse body Palm
Supporting Palm
Windmill Palm
Lying Palm
Returning back Palm
Embracing Palm

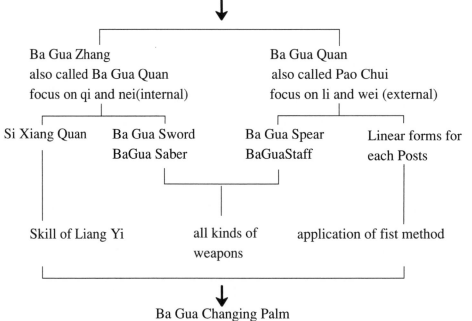

Ba Gua Zhang
also called Ba Gua Quan
focus on qi and nei(internal)

Ba Gua Quan
also called Pao Chui
focus on li and wei (external)

Si Xiang Quan

Ba Gua Sword
BaGua Saber

Ba Gua Spear
BaGuaStaff

Linear forms for
each Posts

Skill of Liang Yi

all kinds of
weapons

application of fist method

Ba Gua Changing Palm

PART 3. BA MU ZHANG POSTURES AND THE EIGHT PALMS

Eight mother palm (Ba Mu Zhang) postures - the previous four palms are to train the basic ability of body ; the first two palms are to integrate the inner ability; the latter two palms are to integrate external ability. The post four palms are to train the four limbs and the body's inter-relationship with up and down , far and near - this is the application .

Ba Gua Quan takes this as the primary method. Thus we know that Ba Gua Quan needs the holistic ability before you talk about application.

name of palm	function	key		description
single changing palm	train qi and li, inner image	inner three harmonies	inner three harmonies	no change to external form , train the qi and li to unify and to separate
double changing palm	train skill and qi, external image	inner three harmonies		change external form, train inner qi and movement together.
Snake palm	contract / expand	outer three harmonies		mainly train elbows, train the ability of the body to expand and contract.
Hook palm	li goes through the ten fingers	outer three harmonies		trains fingers and wrists and all the joints , hooking and grabbing skills.
Closing palm	Upper body palm methods mainly yang-yang.	connect to each other and changing.	outer three harmonies	train applications of upper methods.
Downward flowing palm	swinging palm methods, mainly yin-yin.	(as above)		train applications of lower methods
returning back palm	turning body palm methods, mainly yin-yang.	(as above)		train applications of long range
embracing palm	close body palm, mainly yang-yin	(as above)		train applications of close range.

The eight mother palm postures have no fixed sequence. As long as you keep the key points and attain the function , you can apply the relevant movements or postures in walking the circle or on a straight line. This is also why Ba Gua Quan appears as so many different schools in the past few generations.

After combining the eight mother palm postures and the ba gua, then they appear as eight modes, according to the ba gua position and its features. "Like double changing palm generates eight palm........." . The eight palms are trained according to the human body's inner four organs -(heart, liver, lung , kidney)- and external body parts - (head , back, waist, abdomen).

Single changing palm mainly focuses on pushing palm . It's changing is formless, it's movement's image is different from the other palms changing of forms, but the theory is the same.

Training of the eight trigram palm is by training single changing palm. When you are successful in training the qi and blood, then - according to double changing palm - you practice according to the eight posts. With the eight postures which belong to the eight posts, each takes one animal as a representation to symbolize it's li and qi. It becomes the posture and puts that into the movement.

So we can know that the eight mother palm postures each has it's singular function, and this function can enhance the effect of the inner cultivation . If you take eight mother palm postures according to the change of yin and yang , and use it in each posture, they can help the external effect. So the eight mother palm postures have to be practiced according to the inner four palm's inner cultivation, and the external four palm's yin and yang change, with every posture corresponding with and using each other.

PART 4. External Training and Internal Cultivation

Ba Gua Quan is an art which combines internal and external methods . The pre-heaven qi(body energy) manipulates the post-heaven li (tendons, bones , flesh) , training steel-like strength in the body - this is external training . The pre-heaven qi is led by post-heaven li , gathering peaceful and supple energy to cultivate one's inner nature - this is internal cultivation . The integration of external and internal can lead to endless changes . The procedure of Ba Gua Quan skills follow the circulation of the qi and the blood . It is a very refined and delicate work and links to medical science . The internal cultivation method especially can make the body healthy and the mind peaceful , enabling you to achieve longevity and rid yourself of illness , and it is suitable for all kinds of people to practice .

Ba Gua Quan External Practice Methods

Beginners start to practice the external work of Ba Gua Quan to enhance the bodies energy , make the tendons and bones strong , and to learn how to focus their mind . This is to strengthen the self-nature and the mind .

Mencius said - "If the heaven wants to give someone a big mission it will make him taste the bitter , tax his tendons and bones , make his body hungry and let him have nothing , and yet he will not lose his way . In this way he trains his mind and nature to enable him to do that which he was incapable of before ."

Basic Methods

Ba Gua Quan puts walking first,
This embraces the six harmonies.
Don't be scattered.
Upward and Downward rotate Yin & Yang Palms,
Sink shoulder , drop elbow,
Return to dan-tien.

(Body)

The head and neck are upright , the joint of the neck is in the right position . The chest space naturally sinks , but don't cave in the chest . Sink the shoulders , don't raise them up . Drop the elbows in and close to the body . Qi is stored in the dan-tien and travels vertically in the central channel - don't let it travel horizontally .The six harmonies return to one . If you can do all of this then breathing will be even and regular , natural and long, with qi filling the whole body .

The so-called six harmonies are three internal harmonies and three external harmonies .

Internal harmonies - mind and intention harmonize
intention and qi harmonize
qi and li harmonize
External harmonies - hand and feet
elbows and knees
shoulders and hips

If you have the six harmonies then you can have integrated jin .

(Eyes)

The eyes should focus the spirit and look level as if looking through the crack of a door . The inside is narrow and the outside is broad . Stare at the tip of the index finger . This is the center of focus for your eyesight , so your eyesight moves according to your palm posture . Don't look here and there without concentration . This method can help you to perform the palm skills, which are as follows -

1. Move - seop the adversary inside of your domain.(1)
2. Defend - stop the adversary entering your domain.(2)
3. Hook - lock the adversary's joints.(3)

4. Intercept - attack the adversary's joints . (4-1.4-2.4-3)

5. Push - use short jin to push the adversary and make him lose his balance .(5)

6. Lead the force of the adversary up so that he loses his center of gravity.(6)

7. Bring - lead the adversary's force backwards so that he loses his center of gravity.(7)

8. Throw - use long jin to send the adversary away so that he loses his center of gravity.(8-1.8-2.8-3)

All of these eight methods can have multiple applications , as skills 3-8 can be applied in 1 and 2 , and skills 3 and 4 can be applied in 5 - 8 .

8-1

8-2

8-3

(Palm)

The art of Ba Gua Quan is based mainly on the palm . There are the yin and the yang aspects of the palm . When the center of the palm faces up this is yang , when it faces down this is yin. When the palm raises upwards this is yang , when it stretches downwards this is yin . When the palm stretches forwards this is yang, when it is hidden under the elbow this is yin.

The yin palm index finger points to under the elbow of the yang palm . The root of the yang palm should face upwards with the thumb and index finger open . The li hooks inwards . The center of the palm shape is round and empty , focused inwards . The other three fingers are slightly bent and gathered together , and qi goes through the tips of the fingers .

If the right palm and the left palm are applied then they must change according to the situation in order to help each other . This is called yin and yang combining , and it has various possibilities . Fingers can also vary according to the shape of the palm , no matter whether you attack the adversaries joints or his cavities . Therefore the palm is more convenient to use then the fist.

(Stance)

The stance should be steady and agile .
Stand like a nail
Walk like the wind.
Slightly bend your legs so the height is suitable for moving . Be ready to change with agility , assist the body by the steps , assist the arm by the body, assist the palm by the arm . There is a theory that says , "In Ba Gua Quan , walking is the first thing."

Supple Skills

The purpose of these supple skills is to train the bones to move smoothly and the tendons to be supple. For the bones to move smoothly you must find the right position of the joints. When your blood moves smoothly then your tendons can become supple.

(Rotate wrist)

Take the wrist as the center for the circle. The palm goes right and left and connects two circles like the shape of a figure eight. With your awareness feel your tendons and bones. The photo shows the palm going down, but you must also make the palm go up.1.1-1.8

(Rotate elbow)

There are three ways of rotating the elbow.
1. rotate elbow at front - 2.1 - 2.5
2. rotate elbow at side - 3.1 - 3.8
3. rotate elbow behind - 4.1 - 4.6

These methods rotate the shoulder joints, elbow joints, finger joints, and enhance all the arm-joints range of movement, flexibility and co-operation, stretching the relevant muscles. This rotation of elbow and wrist are the foundation of Ba Gua Quan's changing, twisting and rotation and are very important. These three methods can be practiced seperately or linked.

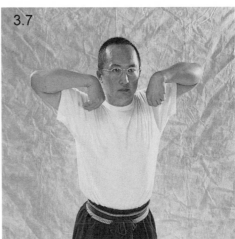

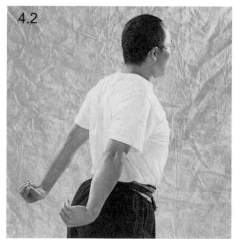

(Rotate waist)

Taking the waist as center, there are two ways of rotating.

1. right and left rotation.

2. spiral rotation.

These methods exercise the spine and waist, and also stretch and extend the back muscles and the tendon and flesh of the back of the leg.

photo 5.1 - 5.8

(Side waist stretch)

The purpose is to enhance the suppleness of the side of the body. When practicing this make sure the horse stance does not move.

photo 6.1 - 6.5

Leg twining

There are three methods for twisting the legs - front , side and back.

Front - the heel of the foot comes close to the body as much as possible but not over the central line, whilst the joint of the hip rotates outwardly and the joint of the knee rotates inwardly. The knees use strength outwardly.

Side - the heel kicks towards the shoulder of the same side of body, and whilst the hip joint rotates inwardly the knee joint rotates outwardly. The knees use strength inwards.

Back - the heel kicks the opposite hip while the hip joint stretches downwards. The knee joint rotates backwards. The knees use strength downwards.

Leg stretching .

Only stretch the legs after warming up. Don't use leg stretching to warm up or else it is easy to be injured. Put one leg to a high place and with the other leg stand up straight. For front, side and back stretching the principle is that the joints must be in the right position.

Front - the tip of the raised leg points to your nose, the leg and kwa make a triangle. The tip of the standing leg faces forwards, and you suck up the crotch. The thigh faces the front and you bend your waist to press your leg. The muscle and tendon being stretched is on the back of the thigh.

Side - the tip of the raised leg points to the ear ,and the leg and kwa become one line. The tip of the standing leg faces forward, and the crotch is in the shape of a vertical triangle. The joint of the thigh is in the side position. Press the leg by the shoulder. This stretches the tendon and muscle of the rear/side of the thigh.

Back - raise the leg and point it to the back of the skull. The leg and kwa are in the shape of a vertical triangle. The tip of the standing leg faces the front. Suck up the crotch. This time the joint of the thigh is in the back position. Press the leg by bending the waist back. This stretches the tendons and muscles of the front thigh and lower abdomen.

Ten Kicking Skills

Leg stretching is still only to stretch the muscles and tendons, but after that you must practice every direction of kicking force. The contents of the ten kicking skills demands stability, you cannot raise up. The upper body doesn't go up or down or lean due to lifting the leg. Ba Gua Quan categorizes the leg exercises as ten skills, the purpose being to practice up and down, horizontal and vertical, and leaning force. The ten skills are explained in the following chart -

skill name	position of contact	jin	attack position
toe kick	top of toes	vertical	private parts, lower jaw, etc.
heel kick	heel	vertical	abdomen, chest, waist, tail bone.
back horse kick	bottom of foot	upwards	private parts.....
tripping leg	lower leg	horizontal	lower leg
catching leg	top of foot	vertical	Ankle, back knee.
short hooking sweep	top of foot	leaning	lower leg.....
big sweep	lower leg	leaning	lower leg, knee, waist...
scissor sweep	lower leg rear/lower leg front	horizontal	lower leg.
stamping kick	bottom of foot	downwards	top of foot
knee strike	knee	vertical	Knee, abdomen, ribs, tail bone...

As for the sequences and postures, the ten skills are in the forms of Ba Gua Quan and will become clear after practice.

The applications are -

Straight leg - kick the leg hard by the method of leg stretching, make the knees straight, this is catching leg.

Thrust kick - lift the thigh first, then stretch the lower leg. Attack forward with the heel. This is heel kick force. Suck up the crotch (dung).

Sole of foot kick - lift the thigh first then stretch the lower leg. Attack sideways by your heel, this is heel kick force. Suck up the crotch.

Back kick - lift the thigh, then stretch the lower leg, attack to the back of your body , this is heel kick force. Suck up the crotch.

Outer crescent kick - the leg lifts up close to the crotch, then draw a curve outwards then down to the side of your shoulder, shaped like a fan. This skill includes knee, catching leg , big sweep , and tripping leg forces.

Inner crescent kick - the opposite of the outer crescent kick .

Jumping inner crescent kick - the center is the hip (like the hub of a wheel), and you jump and rotate the body . Rotate to the left then the left leg does twist outwards step , right leg gwa. After bai tui stand firmly then gwa tui then hold it to become a single posture. The jin is the same as with bai gua.

Inner reaping kick - one leg as the center of circle , then lift the heel as the other leg stretches vertically touching the edge of the circle. The tip of the foot hooks inwards and sticks to the ground , lifting the heel , as the front inner reaping kick draws a circle in a forward direction, and the back inner reaping kick draws a circle by the heel. The upper body is slightly fallen , forming a straight line with the front leg. This includes big sweep, short hooking sweep, toe kick and tripping leg forces.

SIDE PALM

Side palm is for training the ability of the side-body's movement, and it is vital for the variation of twisting.

When you practice side palm, the movements of the hands and legs can't stray out of the shoulder's line.

After completing "preparing posture" and "breathing posture" (referred to in "Ba-Gua internal practice"), follow the photos, then repeat or reverse the practice as in photos 7.1~7.9

7.1

7.2

LOWER PIERCING PALM

"Side palm" and "lower piercing palm" are both kinds of "Changing palm posture".

Due to it's special flexibility, it is used as a warm up.

After completing "preparing posture" and "breathing posture" (referred to in "Ba-Gua internal practice"), follow the photos and practice the left and right sides continuously.

Lowering piercing palm's fixed step training, photos 8.1~8.10

Lowering piercing palm's moving step training, photos 9.1~9.11

LIGHT BODY SKILLS

If you want to be very light and agile, you can only achieve this by first having strong root and stability. If not you will be like the rootless falling leaves and the floating leaves on the water. The stability should be expressed by the lightness and agility, or else you will be stuck like a statue. Ba Gua quan uses many methods to train stability and root - standing like a stake , walking on bricks, running on the wall board, jumping in and out of sandpits, the standing gates, walking on the bamboo basket, and wearing heavy iron weights and sand-filled clothes. Although these are light-body skills they are for training stability.

(Stances)

There is an old saying - "Stand like a stake, walk like the wind".

If we divide the center of gravity of human beings two legs there are three aspects - the middle , the front , and the rear .

This is the same as the steps of Ba Gua Quan - riding horse step , bow and arrow step , and containing chances step .

Every step has it's fixed step and moving step . Here we only teach the fixed step . As for the moving step it should be transmitted by a master since it is very hard to describe using just words.

(Horse Riding Stance)

There are two steps - preparation (photo 10.1) and completed (photo 10.2).

Method

1. For females the step is as wide as the shoulders.
   For males the step is a little wider than the

shoulders.

2. The calf is vertical , not slightly leaning. The knees and ankles take equal amounts of force , and the position of these parts must be correct.

3. The center of gravity is in the kwa . Relax the hips and the waist spine.

4. Sink the waist , sit into the kwa , and suck up the crutch .

5. The shoulders sink and open . The elbows lift and slope downwards. The palms close tightly and push forwards.

6. The head and the eyes look forwards.

7. Upper body sinks to the kwa , let the breathing be natural and deep.

(Bow and Arrow Stance)

Change from horse riding stance to bow and arrow stance (11.3)

Key Points

1. The root of the two legs hook and twist inwards . The front leg goes across (like the Chinese character ding) and the back leg is straight .

2. The inner sides of the thighs stick close together . Inwardly twist the crotch. The hip bone faces forwards.

3. The shin and calf of the front leg are straight . The root of the back leg must not leave the ground , and the force goes down the back leg from the kwa to the foot.

4. The front palm is fixed upright , with the side of the palm pushing forwards. The four fingers are held together with the

tigers mouth (space between thumb and index finger) round and open . The center of the palm sucks in but faces forwards. The tips of the fingers are at nose height .

5. The rear palm index finger points to the front elbow , with the center of that palm facing out and sinking .
6. The two elbows pull inwards and push forwards . The shoulders open backwards.
7. The rest of the key points are the same as for horse riding stance.

12.1 - containing chances stance transition sequence 1.

12.2 - containing chances stance transition sequence 2.

(Contain chances stance)

From a bow and arrow stance into containing chances stance is shown in photos 12.1 to 12.4.

Key Methods

1. Both legs kou inwards towards the crotch. The tips of the toes point forward on one line.
2. The front leg touches the back leg. The hips face forward.
3. The center of gravity goes backwards and sinks down. The lower part of the back leg is in as straight a line as possible. The tip of the front foot points to the ground.
4. The arm and palms are the same as for bow and arrow stance.
5. The rest of the method is the same as for the horse riding stance .

12.3 - containing chances stance transition sequence 3.

12.4 - containing chances stance completion (sitting tiger).

(Bai Kou Step)

Although bai bu (twisting out-wards step) kou bu (twisting inwards step) is the stepping method of the palm movements , actually in Ba Gua Quan the body is assisted by the steps . The steps lead the body which leads the arms which leads the palms , and all of the changing is based on the bai and kou.

1. Bai bu - the leg twists outwards . The tip of the feet point outwards. This is bai bu . If the front leg is bai , then the back leg is kou.

2. Kou bu - The leg twists inwards , with the tip of the foot facing

Left leg bai bu as in photo 13.1   Right leg kou bu as in photo 13.2

inwards, this is kou bu . If the front leg kou , then the back leg can be kou or bai.

3. Bai and kou should be based on the crotch not the foot.

4. In the movement of the bai/kou walking the back leg must touch the front leg. Beginners are required to practice by lifting the back leg higher than the front

leg's knee before stepping. The lower leg is straight and sinks downwards . Put weight into the hips.

(Walking on bricks)

Bricks are an object that the people use in everyday agricultural life . They are easy to acquire, cheap and nice looking. Moreover , bricks have two directions and three dimensions of use. The two directions are length and width , and the three dimensions are flat , sideways , and standing , so in total there are six changes available to practice with . In the later period of standing stake training you must start practicing whilst standing on bricks, but not yet walking . Once you get the strength and you can unify the power of your feet , then you can practice walking . Moreover , only when you are very good at the skill of the walking pushing palm posture should you start walking on bricks .

The early stage of walking on bricks uses twelve to sixteen bricks placed in a circle , and you walk on the bricks using the key points of walking pushing palm . Then the surface area of the bricks becomes smaller and smaller . The sequence is as follows - flat and long , flat and wide , sideways and long , sideways and wide , upright and long , upright and wide .

Because in both "standing on bricks" and "walking on bricks" you don't fix the bricks to the ground , you have an opportunity to examine if the direction of force of your step is right or wrong . The bricks can easily fall down if your step is not steady and rooted . Beginners should practice slowly step by step to prevent injury .

(Running wall board)

In the past the board of gates was very thick and strong , and people would lean this against the wall of the yard and run up and down it . By slowly changing the angle of the board they achieved the desired skill. The skill of flying to a roof and running on walls is from this practice .   The skill of running up the wall emphasizes very fast stepping and "raising the qi" . Also , you learn how to use the force of gravity . If you practice since you are young then from three steps away you can run up a wall . If you start this work after your youth then you may not achieve success .

(Jumping the sandpit)

The inside of a sandpit is very soft so it is not easy to stand still and then jump up . Therefore in the early stage it is necessary to practice "raising the qi" . This is done by standing on flat ground , without bending the knees or ankles , and then making the body jump up . Only with this as a basis can you then start step by step to practice jumping out of the sandpit . Please don't neglect to make the basics of this "raising the qi" strong before you attempt this skill .

(Standing gate)

This is a game played with the gate-board . First , set two gate-boards vertically upright at two side of you , holding one in each hand . Then take your hands off , run fast between them , and before the first board can fall to the ground then you must make it upright again , rapidly turn and stop the second board from falling. The distance of these two gates gets further as your skill gets better . This is a really tough practice !

(Walking the Bamboo Basket)

The shape of the bamboo basket is like a big dish . Gong Bao Tien could walk around the edge of the bamboo basket without falling down . This is the expression of chin-gong , not just a practice .

(Wearing Heavy Clothing)

When you practice the previous skills then you can gradually increase the weight of the body , and this is the point of this particular training . It is better to put weight on the body rather than the limbs . Please do not try this without a teacher's guidance .

TOUGH SKILLS

This training uses hard , heavy objects to train tendons , bones and skins . The utensils used include wooden sticks , wooden men , sand sacks , sand vases , sand bottles , iron hammers , and stone objects . It is easy to get injured doing this type of training so normally it is followed by soft internal exercises and taking a bath in herbal medicine . Don't practice this without a teacher's guidance .

INNER PRACTICE

A practitioner who has a good basis can do the inner practices but without giving up the external training . Inner practices begin with the method of "emptiness" , which is separated into yin and yang aspects . Utilize the items of the Eight palms and integrated with the relevant organs in the body .

Focus very deeply on the lower dan-tien , and send your inner energy through your central channel , making every cavity stable and balanced . Next, circulate your energy and move your palm according to the Eight Posts. Integrate this until you feel the body and spirit unified. The contents of this training are based mainly on single change palm and double change palm . The following are the three steps .

Starting posture
(preparing posture)

Stand upright , shoulders slightly opened and the inside of the two arms touching the body , with the tiger's mouth touching the outer side of the legs . The fingers point straight downwards . The two legs wrap inwards , with the tips of the feet close together and the heels slightly opened . Relax the muscles and absorb the energy into the central channel of the body . The energy will go through the thighs and down to the soles of the feet . The eyesight looks forward and the spirit is concentrated . Empty the mind and breathe out . This is the posture of emptiness . (photo 14)

(regulating breath posture)

1. The shoulders and elbows sink inwardly , the lower arm lifts up , the wrists are relaxed , the thumbs touch the leg and follow the two lines of the ribs upwards . The center of the palms naturally face downwards as they are lifted to the sides of the chest (photo 15.1) . The elbows touch the ribs and do not open outwards .

2. The palms open up with the center of the palms facing forwards . The elbows draw backwards but still close inwards (photo 15.2). Now the palms face downwards , and the qi lifts up to the tip of the lungs . Pause there . Meanwhile the huei-yin(the bottom of pelvis) / shao-fu(lower abdomen) suck up . Your body

inside and outside is drawn up vertically .

3. (photo 15.3) The scapula close inwards and downwards . The chest and abdomen slowly sink . The arms follows this direction and press downwards . The tips of the fingers face forwards . Shao fu - the bottom of this still sucks up energy , and qi is still stored here .

4. Point to note - the purpose of this posture is to restore your organs and jin mai(Qi path) to the right position , so the direction is a vertically upright leading force.

Single changing "palm"

The basic posture in practicing single changing palm is "pushing palm", focusing on li . Turn and walk on the left and the right according to the eight posts . There is a saying - "the steps should be even in single changing palm practice, emphasize the li not the qi". Pushing palm belongs to single changing palm , and it is the original posture of Ba Gua Quan . After you are familiar with the linear forms in the system, you can take pushing palm as the original posture , and connect all the postures in forms and sequences with pushing palm . This is the changing method of single changing palm .

(The Base of Eight Palms - Pushing Palm)

Name of palm - pushing palm
Posture - containing chances posture

Directing: Qi and Li.

1. Relax the waist , move the chest a little forward , sit on the kwa , move the lower belly backwards ; relax your hips, sink the tailbone ; this is all done to open up the centerline which runs from the belly to the chest .
2. Close the crotch area , which makes the Hui-Yin suck up ; store the energy in the belly ; twist your waist to change the pressure of the space in your body and the tension of your tendons ; sink your shoulders , close the arms , open the chest ; all these movements make the jin gather in the center line of the body .
3. Sink the elbow , sink the wrist , set the palm , the center of the palm is inwards , open and round the tigers mouth , make the qi and li penetrate to the tips of the limbs , and integrate the whole body as one .

Jing-Mai(tendon, sinew path) : Take the central channel as the hub which leads all of your body's jing Mai .

1. Lead the jing-Mai section by section , close the shr-da(acupuncture points) by extending muscles .
2. Lead the whole body's jing Mai by the twisting outwards / twisting inwards ,and up and down of the leg , and by the twisting of the waist and the arm , opening and rounding the ten fingers.

Muscle Fibers

1. All the muscles of the body participate in this movement . Feel the fiber of the muscle according to the movement , and consider that the muscle has a downstream and upstream , and that some are moving and some are static .
2. Progressively relax the muscles , enabling the tendons to twist deeply .

Jing Li - Force of Power

1. Pushing Palm belongs to Single Changing Palm and is a method of combining qi and li in order to integrate the jing(power) of the whole body. It is also the roots of the external and internal practices of Ba Gua Quan .

2. Once you are familiar with the turning and stepping , get into the habit of drawing upwards the whole body .

Other points :

1. The early stage of compression is to create pressure from outside to inside . Once you are able to progressively relax your muscles and feel your center line , then it becomes a sucking up power from inside to outside

2. Breathing focuses on the line of the chest and a little to the mid-section.

Photo 16.2 - Pushing Palm Posture upper basin.

The basic posture of Pushing Palm Posture belongs to the middle basin practice. When you are familiar with this then you can expand to upper basin and lower basin practice , applying these basins to train the skills of kuo palm posture.

(Changing Palm Posture)

Energy and blood will be directed into certain areas of the body according to the posture and the direction of walking . This is also the purpose of walking Eight Palm Postures . When you change direction or posture you should not make the circulation of the qi and blood change suddenly , so you need to use some movements that will make the qi and blood follow the sequence of the physiology to certain areas of the body . All of these assisting movements we call Changing Palm Posture .

Photo 16.3 - Pushing Palm Posture lower basin .

(Pushing Palm)

Pushing Palm Posture belongs to Single Changing Palm . When you change the posture the qi and blood continue to

Photo 16.4 - Pushing Palm Posture kou palm.

flow. (Photo 17.1 / 17.2)

17.1 - Pushing Palm Changing Palm Posture 1.

17.2 - Pushing Palm Changing Palm Posture 2.

17.3 - Pushing Palm Changing Palm Posture 3.

17.4 - Pushing Palm Changing Palm Posture 4.

(Lower Piercing Palm Posture)

This posture belongs to the snake palm posture , so you should pay attention to your body and limb's opening and closing , extension and contraction . (Photo 18.1 - 18.9)

(Changing Palm with Lower Piercing Palm Posture)

(Side Palm)

Changing Palm with side palm emphasizes the changing of the force on the left and right sides . Please pay attention to the six harmonies , which are the key points , and to the agility of the kwa and the flexibility of the side of the waist .

(Changing Palm with side palm Photo 19.1 - 19.9)

(Four Postures for Changing Palms)

This is the most formal Changing Palm Posture and the one that is applied the most in the Double Changing Palm Postures . Following are the names of the four postures and their attributes .

1. Green Dragon Turns His Head (also called Dragon Whips it's Tail).
    Generated from Level lifting Palm
    This cleans the energy of the liver .(Photo 20.1 - 20.2)

2. Giant Python Coils it's Body .
    Generated from Windmill Palm .
    This is to relax the waist and abdomen .
    (Photo 21.1)

3. Black Bear reaches out it's Claw .
   Generated from Back Palm .
   To relax and extend the back .
   (Photo 22.1 - 22.3)

4. White Snake Wraps its Body .
   Generated from Lying Palm.
   Cleans up the energy of the heart and lungs .
   (Photo 23.1 - 23.3)

5. push down Palm

Generated from downward flowing Palm .

This is a posture for respiration . It leads the energy of the kidney , and relaxes the tendons and bones under the hip . This belongs technically to the assisting movements , not to the Four Postures . In this example , from the Pushing Palm Posture , both hands from the upper left go towards the lower left , then turn to upper right : this becomes like the Dragon Turn's it's Head right side posture . (Photos 24.1 - 24.3).

The jin of the Four Postures for Changing Palm continues throughout the sequence as if reeling silk from a cocoon , taking care with the transition and changing of the movements . This is "extremely yang becomes yin , extremely yin becomes yang" . The point of the extreme is the point of change .

DOUBLE CHANGING PALM and EIGHT PALM POSTURES

The Double Changing Palm of the Eight Mother Palms mainly trains the co-operation and continuity of the body and inner energy in various postures . In this way external strength is extended towards the relative areas of the body . The primary key point of integrating the internal and external is also the basis of contemporary Ba Gua Quan significance .

Method - Based on the Eight Palm Postures .

Ba Gua Quan is based on the eight trigrams , and harmonized by the five elements . In this way obtain the inner image of the body . This inner image belongs to yi and qi. There is no shape and it cannot be expressed or applied . So Ba Gua Quan selects the movements and images of some representative animals as external images(in order to explain the images by an example). Therefore they will be applied to the object . These external images belong to usage and strength . Ba Gua Quan combines inner images and external images into the palm postures and thus gets Eight Palms , as shown below.

palm name	gua name	gua image	dir.	4 image	5 elements	ext. image	palm posture name	(int. image / domain
Lion Palm	chien	☰	N/W	+ +	fire	lion	lion opens mouth	Head
Downward flowing palm	kan	☵	N	- -	water	snake	white snake slithers through grass	kidney
Back Palm	gang	☶	N/E	+ -	earth	bear	black tiger out of the cave	back
Supporting palm	jun	☳	E	- +	wood	dragon	green dragon coils upward	liver

Windmill Palm	Shing		S/E	- +	wood	roc	huge roc opens it's wings	waist
Lying Palm	li		S	+ +	fire	phoenix	Red phoenix facing towards the sun	heart
Reverse Body abdomen	kuan		S/W	- -	earth	chi-lin	Palmchi-lin spits the book	
Embrace Palm	due		W	+ -	metal	ape	white ape offers fruit	lungs

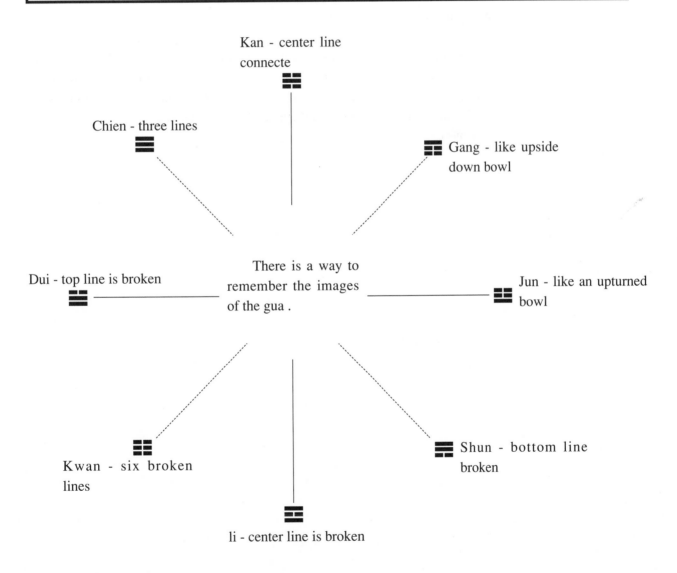

Kan - center line connecte

Chien - three lines

Gang - like upside down bowl

Dui - top line is broken

There is a way to remember the images of the gua .

Jun - like an upturned bowl

Kwan - six broken lines

Shun - bottom line broken

li - center line is broken

The spleen belongs to earth of the five elements , and being the central one of the nine posts it doesn't belong to the eight trigrams . In Ba Gua Quan we train the spleen with the element fire (heart palm) because the heart , spleen and stomach have quite similar positions in the body , and a similarity in the way that their movements interact .

The inner four trigrams belongs to Yin . "Kan , kidney , Jun , liver , Li , fire , Dui , lung". External four trigrams belong to Yang . "Kwan , belly , Shing , waist , Chien , head , Gang , back ."

So the eight trigrams actually come from the Yin Yang side of four images . The eight Palms are also like this .

The Eight Mother "Palms" are the key point of the Ba Gua Quan system . From formless to form , and from mind to practical application , all the following forms , sequences of postures , saber , spear , sword and staff - all of it comes from this training , thus they are called the Eight Mother "Palms".

(map)

Name of palm - lying down palm
Name of posture - red phoenix facing forward to heaven
Gua name - south, li gua , fire ,
Nature - yang yang

To lead your heart and stomach

1. (upward torso) Twist the shoulders backwards and upwards , progressively relax the muscles involved in order to lead the force to go deeper to the domain of the heart and the stomach and even to reach to the depths of the pulse .
2. (downward torso) Follow the twist , the shoulder hooks inwards , the elbow curves outwards , the palm presses downward , the fingertips point forward.
3. Sink the kwa and sit into it .

Jing Mai - leading the heart meridian and pericardium meridian.
The holding arm:

1. The shoulders and elbows turn backwards and lead upwards.
2. The wrists press backwards.
3. The edge of the palm turns backwards.
4. The little finger turns backwards, the middle finger leads forwards.
5. The muscles relax from outside to inside so that the force can go deep.

Muscle

1. The front half of the body stretches the Deltoideus and Pectoralis Major until the Serratus Anterior of the ribs, and the Rectus Abdomini muscles of the belly, with the muscles of the arms and palms twisting in the same direction. Make sure that all the muscles twist in the same direction.
2. Rear half of body - the same as above but in reverse .

Jin Li

1. The Arm drills up, the body sinks down, the tailbone vertebrae relax one by one, and the li of the twist goes from up to down.

Other notes.

1. Although the li goes up your qi should go down, in order that the yin-energy in Li meets the upwards yang-energy in Kan.

2. Why is this posture called "Red phoenix facing forward to the sun?" Because your eyes look a little upwards, and your spirit has to be very open and masculine. The image of this posture is that of a cock crowing in the early morning.

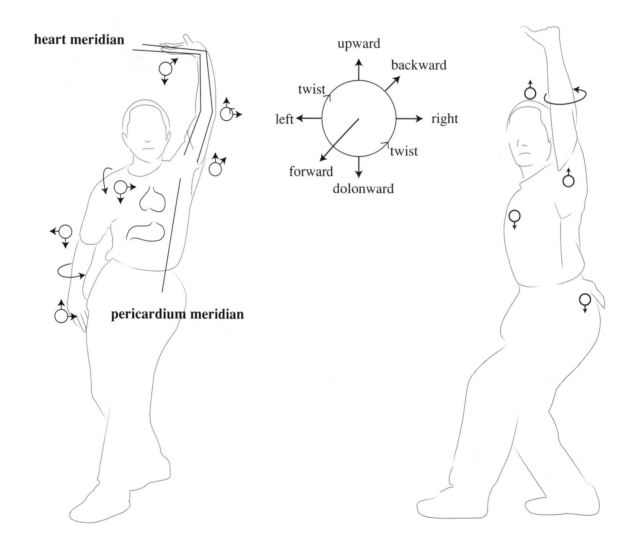

Different images of embracing Palm.
(photo 26,27,28)

Name of Palm - embracing palm
Name of posture - white ape offers the fruit
Gua - west, dui gua, metal.
Nature - yang yin

Leading the energy of the lungs

1. When you do this palm the lungs separate into right and left, with one being closed and one opened.
2. The triceps twists inwardly and stick to the chest, the front shoulder leads backwards, elbow turns up, turn the palm as if holding an object. When you inhale the forward lung breathes in more air and back lung less air.

Jing-Mai - leading Lung meridian

1. The front shoulder leads backwards.
2. The front elbow lifts upwards.
3. The wrist turns sideways.
4. The thumb lifts straight.

Muscles

1. Follow the direction of the Pectoralis Major and Deltoideus muscles, leading them horizontally.

Jin

1. This palm belongs to the horizontal direction and has an opening and closing force. When you close the palm, push forward the Deltoideus leading it horizontally. Do not close that lung.
2. This jin-li is suitable for downward changing force.

Other points

1. The tailbone sinks downwards and backwards.
2. The twist relies on the back arm's push.
3. White ape Offers Fruit is an image of offering something, so the palms push forward whilst the body contracts backwards.

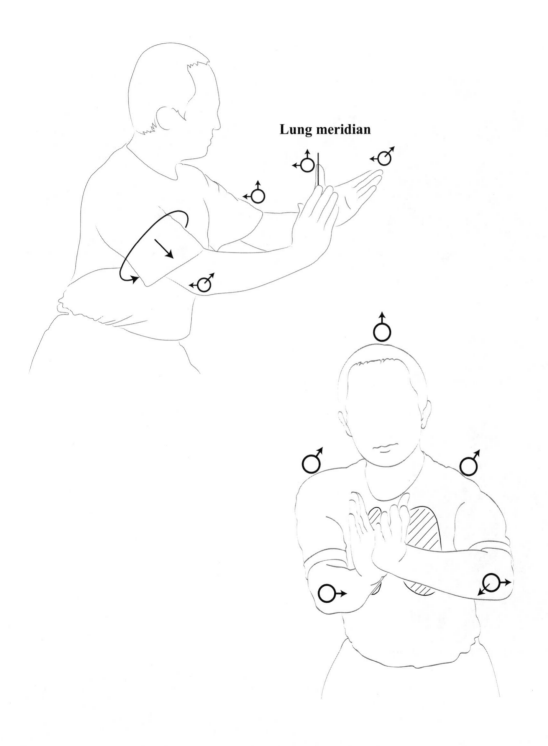

Lung meridian

Different images of embracing Palm.

White Ape Offers Fruit of Ba Gua Quan form.

Mean Tiger Pounds the Heart of Pao-Chui form.

White Ape Offers Fruit of Ba Gua sword form.

Name of Palm - supporting palm
Name of Posture - **green dragon coils upward** (photo 33)
Position of Gua - east , jun , wood.
Nature - yin yang.

Leads the liver .

1. The liver belongs to wood of the five elements and likes to stretch , but because of the influence of emotions and bad posture it is always compressed . This palm opens the ribs allowing the energy of the liver to stretch .
2. The shoulder and the elbow lean up and forward , whilst the waist and kwa sit backwards and downwards . In this way the ribs can open .

Jing-Mai - liver meridian

1. Lead your shoulder and elbow forward
2. Waist and kwa sit
3. The jing shr on legs are lead by twisting steps.

Muscle Fibre

Stretch the front upper body's two muscles Obliquus Major and Serratus Anterior - the direction is side leaning .

Jin

1. The palm's name Green Dragon coils upward is the jin of whirling . It's nature yin yang tells the movement is from low to high .
2. The jin is suitable for upward change .

Other Key Points

1. This posture is for leading the energy of the liver upwards . Don't train your hand with heavy things.
2. The eyesight follows your front palm .
3. The image of this palm is an upwards coiling force . Don't confuse the drilling jin of Lying Down Palm

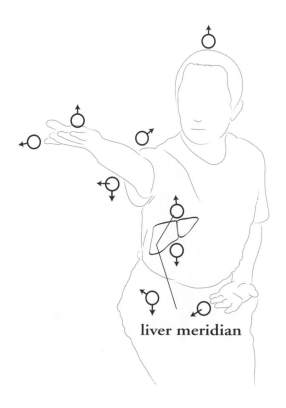

liver meridian

with this one .

supporting Palm also has other images .

Green Dragon coils upward of Ba Gua Zhang form

Single Flamingo flies out of the Crowd of Pao Chui form

Ba Gua sword - Regret the Late Coming of Joy

Name of Palm - downward flowing palm
Name of Posture - white snake slithers through the grass
Gua - north , kan , water.
Nature - yin yin.

37

Leads the Kidney

1. The kidney is like wood on water , if it is too weak it will float up without stability.The elder you become the more your body will be like this. Practice of gong fu requires this special suppression of the kidney . This will make the kidney energy stable .
2. The front shoulder rotates backwards and sinks downwards.
3. The rear shoulder and arm twists inwards .

Jing Mai - kidney meridian

1. Relax the waist , sit into kwa.
2. The shoulder rotates backwards and sinks.
3. Leading the jing-shr of the legs with twisting steps .

Muscle

1. The front upper body muscles Rectus Abdomini muscles and Pectoralis Major leads upwards , going through Deltoideus, towards the back . The back's muscle Grand Latissimus dorsi. , compresses inwards and downwards.
2. Rear body follows the same method but in the other direction.

Jin

1. The downwards force is generated from the rear waist. The force is short and of a yin nature .
2. The force is suitable to be applied upwards and towards the central line of the body.

Other Points

1. Pay attention to the upward leading force of the chest and abdomen , otherwise you will press on the heart and lung and liver .
2. The image of this posture is slithering , so the edge of this palm slips forward and presses downwards like a snake slithering through grass . But this is not

only a pressing force.

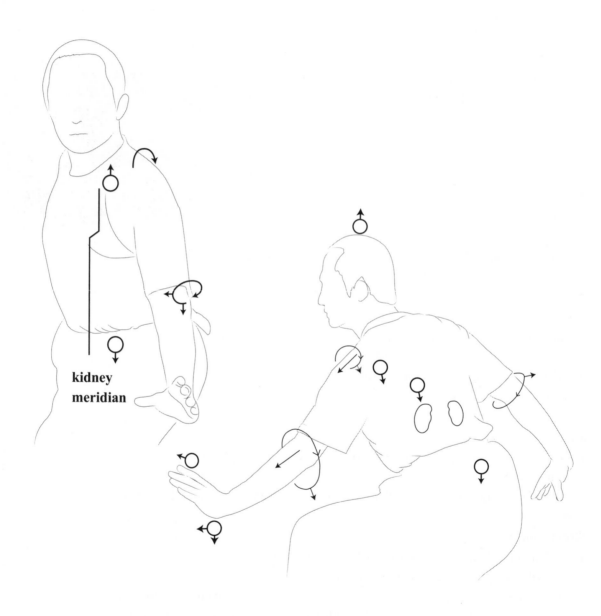

kidney
meridian

Different Images of Following Force Palm

White Ape Offers Fruit of Ba Gua Quan form.

White Tiger Blocks the Road of Pao Chui form

White Snake Slithers through the Grass of Ba Gua Sword

Name of palm -Lion Palm
Name of posture - lion opens his mouth
(photo 41)
Position of gua - west north , chien ,
Nature - yang yang

Direction - head

1. Above the shoulder bone belongs to head .
2. Leading the head upwards , sink your hips downwards , twist your waist in.
3. Stretch all your fingers forward and upwards , the two centers of the palms face each other.

Jing Mai - Small Intestine meridian.

1. The forearms rotate inwards .The rear arm turns outwards and gets close to the ear. The little finger leads forward.
2. The shoulder bone sinks down and closes inwards .
3. The name of the muscle leading upwards - Trapezius.

Small Intestine meridian

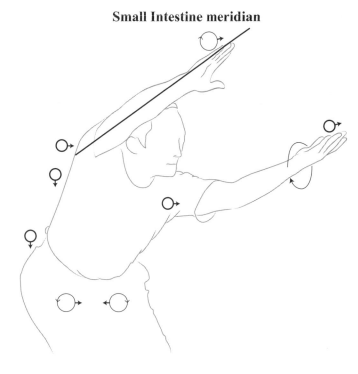

Muscle

Grand Lattisimus dorsi, Deltoideus, Trapezius.................. the muscles from fingers to arms and these muscles all integrate towards the same direction .

Jin Li

1. The force goes upwards through the back of neck
2. Apply with lying palm.

Other points

1. Pay attention to the balance of arms and hips.
2. Pay attention to the distribution of the downward force and upward pulling

force.

3. The purpose of a lion opens his Mouth is to bite and close , so the posture has to have a closing inwards integrated force .

examples of lion palms different images -

lion open his mouth of Ba Gua Quan

face the wind and pierce the sleeves of Pao Chui form

lion opens his mouth of bagua Jien

Name of palm - back palm
Name of posture - black tiger out of the cave
Position of gua , - east north , gang ,
Nature - yang yin

Direction - back

1. Back means the domain of the shoulder bone.
2. The shoulder bone leads to both sides , like a pulling bow in a convex shape.
3. Sink the waist and kwa , the root of the two arms rotates inwards . Don't turn the elbow outwards .
4. This posture has the image of a tigers back.

jing mai............Large Intestine meridian.

1. Leading the index finger forward , slightly sink the wrist.
2. Sink the elbow, rotate the arm inwards .
3. Sink the shoulders , elbows slightly bent and leading forward .
4. Shoulders leading backwards and sidewards .

Muscle

Grand Latissimus dorsi, Pectoralis major, Deltoideus............. these are leading horizontally , the force of the chest slightly backwards , the force of the back slightly forwards .

Jin Li

1. This is a pushing force , taking the back as the root.
2. The back is like a bow , the hands are like arrows .
3. Apply with Embracing Palm .

Other points

1. Don't hollow the chest.
2. The chest and back go in opposite direction , contemplate this carefully.

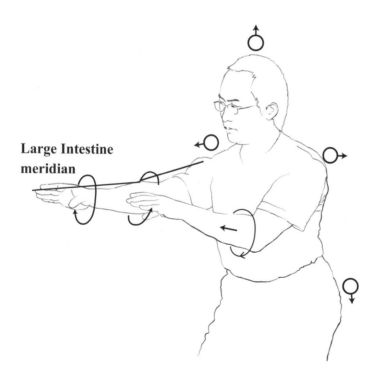

Large Intestine meridian

3. A tigers cave is normally in a high place, so the image of a tiger out of a cave is a force of leaping from upwards to downwards.

example of other postures

Black tiger out of the cave of ba gua quan

Clear away the clouds to see the sun of pao chui

Mean tiger obstructs the road of bagua jien

Name of palm -windmill palm
Name of posture - huge roc opens wings (photo 49)
Position of gua , - south east , shin gua,
Nature -yin yang

Leading the waist

1. The waist is the domain below the shoulder bones and above the hips
2. The front arm turns backwards , back arm turns forward , forming a horizontal force in the waist.

Jing Mai ....Gallbladder meridian

1. The front arm twists backwards . Rotate your shoulder back and downwards .
2. Sink the waist , twisting backwards .
3. Sink the kwa , the tailbone sinks downwards.

Muscles

1. For front arm , the front section of body's Rectus abdomini muscles lead upwards , and Grand Latissimus dorsi of the back contracts downwards .
2. The same but in reverse for the back arm.

Jin Li

1. A twisting force rooted by the waist.
2. The right and left waist simultaneously go in opposite directions .
3. Apply with supporting palm .

Other points

1. Don't move the belly due to the twisting of the waist.
2. In this posture the left and right body parts go in different direction , so contemplate this carefully.
3. The image of this posture is open because this bird is huge , the wings fold and unfold in a certain sequence ,so you should be aware of the sequence of the

twisting and turning force.

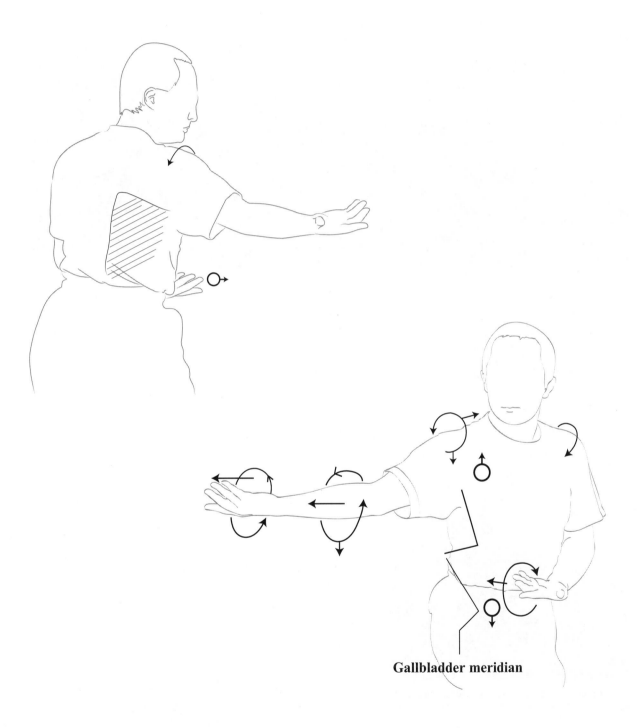

Gallbladder meridian

Other images of windmill palm

Big roc opens its wings of Ba Gua Quan

Open the window and look at the moon of pao chu

Lying down and looking at the seven stars constellation of Ba gua jien

Name of palm -Reverse body palm
Name of posture -Chi lin spits the book
Gua - south west , kwun trigram
Nature - yin yin

Leading the abdomen

1. This includes the domain beneath the diaphragm and above the hip bones.
2. Relax the abdomen , make the qi sink.
3. Both arms embrace like a circle , lift the center of the palms .
4. Release the chest but don't close it . The shoulder nest doesn't go in.

Jing Mai - Bladder meridian

Relax the abdomen , the head raises up , sink the tail-bone .

Muscles

Relax and drop the muscles of the chest and abdomen . The muscles of the waist and back naturally pull upwards .

Jin Li

1. The force of this posture is from the lower part of the abdomen and from the spitting jin of the back .
2. Apply with downward flowing palm.

Other points

1. The belly stays inwards , don't push it out.
2. This posture has the meaning of returning to the origin, so it is mostly practiced before you finish training .
3. In the legend, the book Luo-Shu was carried by the "chi lin" animal , and this posture is also called chi-lin spits his whiskers . This means you use your fingers to pierce like whiskers , but the main point is to motivate the abdomen's splitting force .

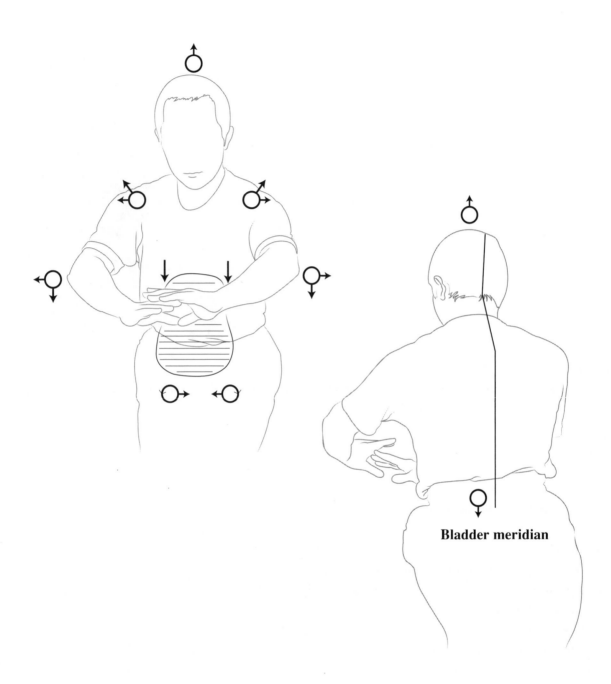

Bladder meridian

Different images

Chi-lin spits the book

Rotating yin yang palms of pao chui form

chi lin spits the whiskers of Ba Gua Jien

Eight Palms Circle Walking

The purpose of the circle walking eight palms is to find the correspondence between external movement and internal force . The beginning posture is like Single Changing Palm but has it's focus on qi. There is a song , "circle walking eight palms , qi has to be refined , so focus on qi not li" . Thus when you move , start from the Single Changing Palm , and after walking clockwise and counter-clockwise change this posture into the other palms by "Changing Palm Posture" . The sequence would be - heart , lungs , liver , kidney , head , back , waist , abdomen . Leading the inner qi by external force motivates the external li by inter-nal qi, they interact with each other until qi makes the li move . After the Eight Palms return to pushing palm and walk for one circle . After making the heart peaceful and the energy harmonious regulate the breathing and finish the exercise .

(Embracing Palm change with Lower Piercing Palm)
Example - as photo 57.1 to 57.8.

(Lion palm change with the four postures for changing palm)
Example - as photo 58.1 to 58.13.

(Windmill palm change with the side palm)
Example - as photo 59.1 to 59.14.

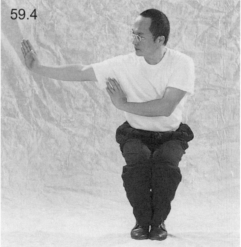

PART 5. APPICATIONS

Examples of spontaneous responses to unplanned attacks by a baguaquan expert. The photos are self-explanatory, but here we explain some of the key concepts and tactics used by Master He.

series 1

In this sequence of exchanges Master He demonstrates the concepts of simultaneous defence and attack (photo 2), folding (in photo 3 his arm is trapped so he folds and hits with the elbow), and bai-bu/kou-bu (in photo 7 he swiftly uses these steps to encircle and follow the attacker in order to subdue him with a painful arm lock).

series 2

The attacker pulls Master He directly backwards and down, but Master He simply yields , twists and moves in with his own attack to both the face and the leg. Note how he falls onto the attacker's body and right leg, effectively unbalancing him and preventing further strikes.

series 3

Against a grab from the side Master He steps deeply into the attackers root with an elbow strike, persuing him until a powerful punch sends him flying. This is typical of Baguaquan's tactic of moving the whole body in, not being 'stuck on the spot'.

series 4

A bear hug from the rear that traps the arms is difficult to escape, but here Master He uses "bone to bone" power to loosen the grip (photo 2). He then sends a deep twist through his torso, the effect of which is very clear as the attacker flies off.

series 5

The attackers initial low punch is met with a simultaneous deflection and low kick, and he is forced to step back. Immediately Master He persues him with lower piercing palm and launches a leg attack which sends the attacker sprawling.

series 6

Master He stops the first low punch, but allows the second strike to come very close so that he can trap the arm and simultaneously use a piercing palm strike to the throat. Note how his body and step once again move in, forcing the attacker backwards.

series 7

This illustrates the same principle of trapping as in the last sequence, but this time against a frontal grab. Note how a baguaquan expert will sometimes purposefully expose a vital area (in this case the face) to lure the attacker into a trap.

series 8 - kick defence

against front kick master He instantly evades and steps in with right elbow strike.

series 9- against close range attack master He moves in and jams the attacker's space. Alex evades the counter attack with a step but master He keeps on following until at last he takes Alex's center, spins around very fast and strikes with elbow. Alternative ending is to throw with a spinning action.

series 10- against a series of strikes master He drops to ground and delivers two kicks from a low position.

series 11 - umbrella

Alex attacks and Master He uses his umbrella to keep him at a distance, moving his body just enough to be out of range. Each time Alex attempts to grab or stop the umbrella, Master He changes the line and using spiral motion attacks from a different line. Finally the attacker is trapped and unable to move further. This

series uses the principles found in the sword training.

PART 6. AUTHOR'S POSTFACE

Since the old times Ba Gua Quan is a small group , with not only few teachers but also few students . Along with the few people who can deeply understand the whole system , because of destiny not many can get a glimpse of the art and are willing to strive to study , write and spread the knowledge without concern for the cost . Because of this , and since I have entered the precious mountain , I don't want to leave without a harvest . I also feel a responsibility to share the knowledge with more and more people .

Even the publisher , Mr. lio , did not worry that this book has a narrow market and may be difficult to earn money from , so he is willing to publish a series of Ba Gua Quan books . I was surprised and touched by that . A new age is coming . Everybody has been perceiving consciously the special character of the 21st century which is an explosion and proliferation of information ,a merging of careers , global family , and so on . Under these circumstances how should the individual respond to this and yet still keep his own particular values and sense of judgment ? It is extremely vital and yet most people don't consider this point.

Ba Gua Quan gives abundant experiences in self-mastery for an individual's ability with body and mind , and contains a thorough training procedure to strengthen and adjust the body and mind . I hope people can acknowledge the worth of Ba Gua Quan , or we can say Chinese martial arts education , and in this way make Ba Gua Quan continuously serve contemporary and future human beings with it's unique essence .

This series of books is just an introduction for guidance to the art . The ancestors have said , "Only method or Dharma is not enough by itself". Similarly the art also need human beings to participate in it's practice , and then it will start to be alive .

Are you willing to make effort for your health of body and mind?

Are you willing to prepare and welcome the challenge of the next century?

Are you willing to be the example and positive proof for the next generation?

Are you willing to become a creator of Ba Gua Quan's life?

You need Ba Gua Quan !
Ba Gua Quan needs you!

PART 7. Glossary of Chinese Terms

Ba Gua - 八卦

The eight trigrams , or sets of three broken and unbroken lines , which are an important symbol in Taoist practices.

Ba Gua Quan - 八卦拳

Eight Trigram Boxing , the term used by the Yin Fu and particularly the Gong Bao Tien descendents of the Master Dong Hai Chuan.

dung - 襠

Crotch area .

dung power - 襠勁

An archlike structure of the tendons and sinews in the crotch area.

gong fu - 功夫

The result of concentrated effort over a long period of time , often used to describe the skill of an expert martial artist - "he has gong fu".

jin - 勁

A particular kind of power or ability , with each martial art specializing in certain types of "jin".

jing - 筋

The system of tendons , sinews and soft tissue in the human body.

jing-lo - 筋絡

The tendon / sinew pathways.

kua - 胯

The area running from the crotch , through the inside of the hip cavity and the inguinal region.

nei-gong - 內功

Training methods which work the parts of the body and energy not normally under concious control.

qi - 氣

Energy , life force inherent in all things , bio-electrical current in the human body.

qi gong - 氣功

Methods of working with the life force , often related to working with the breath.

qi-mai - 氣脈

the pathways along which qi flows in the human body, often referred to as meridians.

tao - 道

the Way , a path .

tao-lu - 套路

a form , a sequence of martial arts movements having a specific purpose and structure.

Taoism - 道家

the original spiritual / religious Way of ancient China , now existing in many forms - ie. religious Taoism , folk Taoism , Taoist martial arts etc.

wai-gong - 外功

methods to develop the external structure and power of the martial arts student.

yang - 陽

the active , emissive principle in the Universe.

yin - 陰

the passive , absorbing principle in the Universe.